Praise for *A Chance to Say Goodbye* ...

Part tribute, part memoir, part guide, *A Chance to Say Goodbye* succeeds on all counts, with lyrical writing and thorough research... In recounting her father's story, Shultz enables readers to share in her loss. And she offers a wealth of practical advice on everything from writing an obituary to clearing out a house... Thought provoking and absorbing, *A Chance to Say Goodbye* has much to offer readers willing to confront the challenging subject of end-of-life.

~BlueInk Review
★ Starred Review

Shultz is a self-critical guide through the process of loss, but she also seems to find some peace in the idea that her insights might help others to make healthier choices. Communication stands out as an essential tool, and Shultz's preparatory notes are full of sage advice. Prose is clear and direct, and the end result is both reflective and encouraging. *A Chance to Say Goodbye* is a heartfelt, moving reminder that loving words are never wasted. In its personal nature, it makes convincing arguments against risking regret."

~Foreword Clarion Review, ★★★★

This personal narrative of a universal experience is both touching and useful. Lisa gently guides the way through navigating the death of a parent, an experience many will face but few will be prepared for. Her honesty on a difficult topic is refreshing. After reading this book, I feel more confident in facing what lies ahead.

~Gwen Van Velsor, Author of *Follow That Arrow*

This book is deeply personal and insightful. You're sure to gain valuable knowledge as well as important tools and resources from Lisa's exceptional book. She offers honest emotions from her experience. I also enjoyed getting to "know" her father as a vibrant and healthy man, prior to his failing health. A must read!

~Kate Heartsong, Author of *Deeply We Are One*

A Chance to Say Goodbye is a book anyone who has aging parents needs to read. The experience of parenting a parent through medical, financial, and even the issues of daily living can be so frustrating and isolating. Read Lisa's book and you'll know you're not alone. You'll gain key understanding for the time when you are about to enter this phase with a parent. Insightful and beautifully written!
~Gayla Wick, Author of *The Art of Attracting Authentic Love*

Lisa shares a touching life experience in *A Chance to Say Goodbye: Reflections on Losing a Parent*. Part memoir, part historical documentary, part tutorial on aging and dying, this wonderful work does not leave anything out in preparing for the journey of losing a loved one. Her thorough research gives the reader many resources to consider and her well-chosen quotes comfort, inspire, and challenge one's spirit for the time they begin this difficult journey. Death is a natural part of Life's progression, and Lisa helps the reader navigate this season with much tenderness and honesty.
~Connie Pshigoda, Author of *The Wise Woman's Almanac: A Seasonal Guide with Recipes for New Beginnings that Never Go Out of Season*

A Chance to Say Goodbye is a labor of love and a must read. The author tells a heartwarming and heart wrenching account of her relationship with her father. In today's society, we avoid thinking of the later years in our relative's lives. This book should remind all adult children with aging parents that they must prepare for their loved ones' future as well as their own. Thank you, Lisa!
~Karen Owen-Lee, Author of *The Caring Code and The Caring Crisis*, CEO and founder of Housing Options for Seniors, Inc.

Full of resources and insights, *A Chance to Say Goodbye* is a helpful read for anyone navigating the journey with an aging loved one. The section on the caregiver's own grieving process is just as helpful as how to talk to your loved one about their impending death.
~Jan Haas, Author of *Moving Mountains: One Woman's Fight to Live Again*

If you are in the sandwich generation, you need this book. Lisa Shultz's honest, compassionate, and compelling exploration of her own reactions in assisting her dad to complete his life make the process of caring for and losing an aging parent unflinchingly real. The resources she discovered and shares will help you prepare to meet the inevitable challenges that arise when you assume similar responsibilities.

~Dr. Laurie Weiss, Author of *Letting It Go: Relieve Anxiety and Toxic Stress in Just a Few Minutes Using Only Words*

This is an outstanding book about Life, Death, and Caretaking. Beginning with a biography of her father, *A Chance to Say Goodbye* is not just a memoir, but rather sets the scene for her experiences and frustrations as her father's caregiver at the end of his life. She gently explains her experience as daughter and supervisor of his final years. Finally, Lisa masterfully moves into 'how to mode' and gives a detailed blueprint of the steps each of us might follow to prevent the difficulties she experienced. A worthwhile book about a very difficult subject, it is beautifully written, interesting, and personal, moving the reader effortlessly though the frustrations of caretaking, dying, and death. After reading it, you will be grateful to Lisa Shultz for her insights on this sensitive subject.

~Rhondda Hartman, Award Winning Author of *Natural Childbirth Exercises for the Best Birth Ever* and *Natural Childbirth Exercise Essentials*

With captivating transparency, Lisa Shultz shares fun memories, uncertainties, fears, emotions, and challenges of becoming the caregiver, watching her father slowly weaken. The insights and lessons learned will prove valuable to those being cared for as well as those involved with end-of-life matters on behalf of a loved one. The resources and questions Lisa includes will be helpful to anyone facing such decisions.

~Ted Dreier, Author of *Take Your Life Off Hold*

A Chance to
Say Goodbye

A Chance to Say Goodbye

Reflections on Losing a Parent

Lisa J. Shultz

A Chance to Say Goodbye: Reflections on Losing a Parent
Published by High Country Publications
Breckenridge, CO

FIRST EDITION
2017

Library of Congress Control Number: 2017933093

Shultz, Lisa J., Author
A Chance to Say Goodbye: Reflections on Losing a Parent
Lisa J. Shultz

ISBN 978-0-9986509-0-6
1. SELF-HELP / Aging
2. FAMILY & RELATIONSHIPS / Eldercare
3. FAMILY & RELATIONSHIPS / Death, Grief, Bereavement

Book Design and Cover Design © 2017
Cover and Interior Design by Andrea Costantine
Editing by Donna Mazzitelli, The Word Heartiste
Author photo by Tamara Murphy-Webb
Interior photos courtesy of the Shultz family archives

To my dad
Robert V. Shultz
1925-2015

"Take the very hardest thing in your life,
the place of difficulty, outward or inward,
and expect God to triumph gloriously in that very spot.
Just there He can bring your soul into blossom."
From *Parables of the Cross* by Lilias Trotter

Contents

Foreword

Throughout my medical career as a hospice doctor and a writer I have collected and cherished stories of the beautiful transformations that occur at the end of life: when patients, whose physical suffering has been well-managed, find meaning and purpose in their own dying process, when family members reconcile and reunite in love, when care providers are reminded why they do this important work of shepherding patients through the dying process. I have thrived on stories such as this and, indeed, have been inspired to change the way I live my own life and to share the possibility of transformation through dying in my own writing. In contrast to these beautiful stories, however, the most painful encounters I have experienced have been those situations when a patient "falls through the cracks" between the best intentions for medical care and the flawed delivery system that prevents those intentions from being made a reality.

When I sat with Lisa Shultz over coffee one afternoon and heard the details of her father's last months of life and her own anguish as one of his caregivers during that process, I recognized that this was an example of the failure of our health system to provide adequate end-of-life care for an elderly patient. I also knew that this was a story of equal, if not greater, importance than every transformative story I have ever told. Through my medical training I have learned that often the best education can be found in situations where things have not gone as well as hoped and where lingering questions have given way to doubt, guilt, remorse, or pain. These stories (or "case studies" as we call them in medicine) become cautionary tales that point out the gaps in care that exist despite our best efforts and sincere desires to do the right thing.

In her book *A Chance to Say Goodbye: Reflections on Losing a Parent,* Lisa Shultz offers a candid and unflinching look at the end of her father's life and the many gaps in care, decision-making, communication, and a culturally-influenced mindset that made his dying process far more difficult than necessary for everyone involved. Shultz's experience has been echoed by other contemporary authors, including Dr. Atul Gawande, who revealed the brokenness of our healthcare system through the story of his own father's death in his book *Being Mortal.* Similarly journalist Katy Butler in *Knocking on Heaven's Door* explored the challenges of helping her parents create a "good death" within our current medical model.

So too in caring for her father, Lisa Shultz confronted medical providers that not only did not meet his or her family's needs but also did not even acknowledge or understand those needs. As the story unfolds in *A Chance to Say Goodbye*, she describes each scenario clearly and depicts how one failure of communication after another led to her father receiving treatment that, in retrospect, was ill-advised and diminished the quality of his life during his last days.

However, the book offers a saving grace within this otherwise tragic tale: it lies in Shultz's ability to rise above her own grief and remorse and thoughtfully reflect on the driving forces behind this event. She analyzes the factors in her father's own history and personality that contributed to his reluctance to talk about the end of life. She explores the difficulty she encountered when trying to communicate with him or his doctors about death and the general lack of knowledge and information about dying that prevented her from seeking additional assistance. Each of these issues compounded the others and created the untenable end-of-life scenario that the book describes; a story that is unfortunately repeated every day in hospitals and long-term care facilities across this country.

Ultimately, Shultz achieves her goal of educating and informing readers so that they might avoid a scene such as this in their own or a loved one's dying process. She offers resources and recommendations to help other non-medical caregivers navigate the healthcare system and create the conversations needed to guide the best possible decision-making. With the writing of *A Chance to Say Goodbye*, Lisa Shultz has found a way to light the path through the end-of-life process for patients and their loved ones. As a result, she brings meaning and purpose to her father's death and to her own grief as well.

Over the years, I've learned that facing the pain of our inadequacy is the first step toward growth and evolution. Lisa Shultz has shown us the pain that occurs when our medical system doesn't recognize death as a necessary aspect of the cycle of life and when we, as individuals, ignore death rather than prepare for our last days. This is our first step toward evolving a healthcare system where the end of life is given as much attention as the beginning and a society where death is discussed and planned for as a normal part of life. It is time to bridge the gaps so that no other patient or loved one "falls through the cracks." The goal of this book is one that really matters: it can change our entire society for the better and allow everyone "a chance to say goodbye" with those we love.

Karen M. Wyatt MD
Author of *What Really Matters:*
7 Lessons for Living from the Stories of the Dying
Silverthorne, Colorado 2017

Introduction

"When we are no longer able to change a situation,
we are challenged to change ourselves."
Victor Frankl

As I entered my late forties and early fifties, I was caught off guard. When I was younger, I looked to the future and saw my role as wife and mother, but I didn't foresee being a shepherd to my parents as they aged. I had not observed my mom and dad caregiving for their parents, and I did not have personal friends in that role at the time. When my dad's health began to fail, I didn't know what to do.

Completely unprepared for this new position, I found myself in the phase of life referred to as the sandwich generation. My dad needed my attention and so did my growing daughters. I was immersed in the tasks and management of hospitalizations and rehabilitation for my dad while also handling the responsibilities as mother to my two daughters—and all of this as I simultaneously strove to maintain my own life. I felt stretched by the needs of three generations—myself in the middle.

Although I have three older siblings, for a variety of reasons I ended up accepting the role of primary decision maker. My brothers live in South Dakota, making it difficult for them to visit often. My sister and I both live in Colorado, so due to our proximity to our dad, we were most involved. My sister was proficient in handling my dad's accounting, bills, and tax preparation. I had a medical background as a former physical therapist, so my siblings looked to me to navigate the medical aspects of my dad's care. Additionally, I had the most flexible schedule, since I did not have a traditional job.

As primary decision maker, I had tough choices to make, such as selecting a rehabilitation facility and later a skilled nursing unit, as well as decisions about signing a DNR (Do Not Resuscitate order). I had to constantly consult with doctors, nurses, and therapists regarding my dad's progress and future plans. There were numerous medical team meetings to attend, paperwork to sign, and frequent updates to provide to my siblings. I learned how to manage the ever-changing situation and anticipate necessary decisions by blundering through each with a firm resolve to do my best. At times the responsibility felt heavy and overwhelming, yet I pushed through the tough times knowing that eventually my role would change.

My dad passed away on October 31, 2015, at the age of eighty-nine. His remarkable life had concluded, but initially I did not feel a sense of closure and completion. Because I was not at his bedside to say goodbye at the time he died, my relationship with my dad felt unfinished. It took time to find peace in the knowledge that I had been unable to be with him at such a significant moment.

It turned out there was even more that felt unresolved. I'd felt at odds with the medical culture I encountered, which avoided conversations about death. Pride, denial, and fear seemed to permeate my dad and the western medical establishment that surrounded him. This stance did not seem to serve him or our family well, which resulted in unnecessary suffering for everyone.

During the months after my dad's death, I began journaling and sifting through memories as a way to digest and make sense of all that had transpired during his decline. I found that it was not enough for me to just sign off and say, "Been there, done that, job over." I couldn't just tell myself that now that my dad was gone, I could go back to life as usual. I felt unsettled, sensing there might have been a better way to conclude my dad's life. Here was a man who had been a World War II veteran—an individual who lived an incredible life until his health diminished.

I am not an investigative journalist, but I began searching for books, articles, and resources that might help me understand more about the end of life and options for end-of-life care and treatment. Knowing that I was born at the tail end of the Baby Boomer* generation, I suspected that some of my peers had written about their experiences.

The first book that opened my eyes to decisions about end-of-life care was *Knocking on Heaven's Door* by Katy Butler. She began the book by telling about her mother who asked her to help turn off her father's pacemaker. The

---

* Baby Boomers are the demographic group born during the post World War II baby boom, approximately between the years 1946 and 1964. https://en.wikipedia.org/wiki/Baby_boomers

concept of keeping his heart beating when it was time to die had become too much for her mother to bear. I was in the midst of reading this book when my dad began to exhibit signs that indicated his heart was failing. I had read enough of her book to realize that choices made to prolong his life at that stage in his decline would not serve anyone well, most especially him.

The subtitle to Butler's book is *The Path to a Better Way of Death*. The concept of a good death or bad death was seeded in my mind as I began to witness my dad's complications of infection and pneumonia from a surgery he underwent to remove his gall bladder. My dad did not have a pacemaker, but learning from Katy Butler's experience and unpleasant tale, I recognized the perils in prolonging life. I felt that at some point in a deteriorating health scenario, it is a mercy to allow the body to quit. Rather than viewing death as a failure or the result of giving up, dying might be seen as a natural progression. Battling the cycle of life, especially a long and well-lived life, seemed cruel.

I read numerous books about good deaths and bad deaths and consider my dad's death somewhere in the middle of the good and bad scale. It could have been much worse. He ended up dying alone in the skilled nursing wing of a rehabilitation facility. I have heard that some people prefer to die alone as a way of sparing their loved ones from witnessing their last breath. I am not sure if my dad made that choice or if his heart just stopped when no one was in his room. From what the nurses told me, he died peacefully.

Because I was not satisfied with the way my dad's amazing life concluded, I decided to dig into the experience. I asked myself, "If I had known at the beginning of the story how it

would turn out in the end, what would I have done differently?"
I looked back and looked within to find answers. Several
months after my dad passed, I felt an urge to chronicle our
story. I began with recording our histories. Simultaneously,
I read books that friends recommended or that came up in
my internet searches. I became aware of authors who were
doctors, hospice workers, and ordinary people like Katy Butler
who felt compelled to share their experiences of death. Often
their views were shaped by difficult circumstances.

In the same way I imagine a researcher goes about their
work, I gathered together all of what I discovered. I wrote
pieces that would later become chapters. I printed out each
section and laid everything across my dining room table. I
pondered how to put the information together in a meaningful
way. I moved the puzzle pieces around in an effort to highlight
the struggles we experienced.

This book is not a commemoration of my dad, but I
strove to honor him. I intended to be considerate of him, his
friends, and my family. Sharing details of dying and death is
sometimes taboo and often difficult to read and discuss. I
chose to publish our experience to potentially lessen suffering
for caregivers and their aging loved ones.

The large gap in my knowledge of the dying process for
an elderly parent has narrowed. I am also now keenly aware of
my own mortality and believe that I have the opportunity to
adjust and create my life with a focus on quality over quantity.
Understanding that each person's experience of death and
dying is as unique as the personalities of those involved, I
learned a great deal when I read other individuals' accounts
of losing a loved one. That knowledge led me to the desire
to share our story.

After the historical and memoir sections of *A Chance to Say Goodbye*, you'll find a list of writings I discovered as well as how they continue to impact my thoughts and goals. You'll also find additional tips, suggestions, and resources to assist you and your family as you navigate end-of-life circumstances and decisions.

Wherever you find yourself with regard to end-of-life matters, may you find guidance, support, and ultimately peace in your journey.

PART ONE

A Storied Life

"Life is not that which one lived, but that which one remembers, and how one remembers to tell it."
Gabriel Garcia Marquez

CHAPTER ONE

Shultz Family History

*"We all grow up with the weight of history on us.
Our ancestors dwell in the attics of our brains as they do in the
spiraling chains of knowledge hidden in every cell of our bodies."*
Shirley Abbott

B obby, as he was affectionately called, was the only child to Jane Elizabeth Brown and Ralph Leonard Shultz. His given name was Robert Vernon Shultz, and he was born on December 10, 1925. In that year, Calvin Coolidge was president of the United States, the Charleston was the dance craze, and women wore flapper style clothing. Adolf Hitler published *Mein Kampf* and F. Scott Fitzgerald

Baby Bobby

published *The Great Gatsby*. Orchestras such as Paul Whiteman and Ray Miller were popular. Charlie Chaplan's film, *The Gold Rush*, was a hit, as was *The Big Parade* and *Ben-Hur*. My dad shared his birth year with Paul Newman, Malcolm X, Dick Van Dyke, and Johnny Carson. Gasoline was twelve cents per gallon and a postage stamp was two cents. Life expectancy was 54.1 years.*

1859 Schultz Family in Germany

The Shultz family (originally spelled Schultz until the "c" was removed around the turn of the twentieth century) came from Schleswig, Germany. Peter Schultz, my dad's grandfather, was born in 1849 and sailed across the Atlantic Ocean in 1865 with his parents and three brothers when he was sixteen years old. He married his first wife, Wilhelmine Gethman, in 1870 and had four children with her. He learned a new language and began to assimilate into his new country, residing in Iowa.

---

* 1925 Remember When Kardlet http://www.seekpublishing.com/public/

At that time, pioneers were heading west with the promise of being able to stake a claim on the land there. In 1882, Peter moved his family to Dakota Territory, which was ultimately named South Dakota when it officially gained statehood in 1889. His wife died shortly after the move in 1883. Peter then married Caroline Hildebrand in 1884. Together they had eight children, and their sixth child

Peter Shultz

was Ralph Shultz, born in 1897. Ralph was my dad's father.

Peter was a bona fide pioneer. His land claim in Viola Township was in central South Dakota, where land was used for ranching and agriculture. During the subsequent forty years after he arrived in the region, Peter raised his large family, built a significant estate, retired, and moved from his farm to the nearby town of Wessington Springs in 1907. Peter then became involved in the local government. He was the mayor of Wessington Springs when he died in 1926.

On the maternal side of my dad's family, his mom, Jane Brown, applied to the National Society, Daughters of the American Revolution. She traced her ancestry back to Henry Hostetter, born in 1760, who fought in the Revolutionary War, acting in the capacity of First Lieutenant 6th Class York Co. Militia.

My dad's mother, affectionately called "Brownie," moved to South Dakota from Indiana and began teaching in a school located in Aurora County, twenty miles south of Wessington

Ralph and Jane Shultz

Springs. She stayed at the home of Ellen and Sam Stuck, who lived on a farm a mile or so from the one-room schoolhouse where she taught. It wasn't long before the Stucks had a Sunday dinner for their relatives, which included Ellen's brother Ralph. Ellen arranged the seating and placed Jane and Ralph together. The strategic placement worked, and the two began to court each other until they were married in Wessington Springs on June 18, 1924.

Baby Bobby with mother and father

It was a tough year to begin their marriage, because Ralph and Jane's farm buildings were destroyed by massive tornados that same year. However, the following year brought good fortune, when my dad, their only son, Robert Vernon Shultz, was born.

Most of my dad's childhood was uneventful. He and his parents lived on a 320-acre stock farm in Viola Township in South Dakota, raising cattle, hogs, chickens, and a few milk cows. My dad attended a one-room schoolhouse until the fourth grade, when his folks moved to Wessington Springs, a nearby town, which at that point had a population of approximately 1,400. The severe draught and grasshopper infestation of the early 1930s forced his parents to sell their farm in April 1934. His parents purchased a small hardware store, which they called "Shultz Hardware," and lived above the store on Main Street.

Bobby about age 3

In high school, my dad's nickname was "Scoop," because he was the sports editor of the weekly paper and yearbook during his junior year. In his senior year, he was Editor in Chief. He also enjoyed playing sports in high school, which included track, basketball, and football.

Bob in High School

He was a junior in high school and turned sixteen years old three days after the Japanese attack on Pearl Harbor, December 7, 1941. It would be

Bob in the Navy

two more years before he could volunteer for service or be drafted. Everyone looked up to servicemen at the time, and when they came home on furlough from the army or leave from the navy they were considered heroes. The newspapers and newsreels at the movie houses, popular music, and personal conversations were dominated by the war.

Since he was only seventeen-and-a-half when he graduated from high school in 1943, my dad had to wait until later in the year to enlist. A few weeks before he turned eighteen, on December 10, 1943, he was told that if he volunteered for the draft, he would be given his choice of branch of the armed forces in which to serve. He was anxious to get in and disappointed that his eyesight kept him out of Army Air Corp or Officer's Candidate school. Since several of his classmates had gone into the navy, my dad and two of his buddies requested that branch of the services.

After a trip to the induction center near Sioux City for physicals and tests, my dad caught a train to Farragut, Idaho, for boot camp. Following boot camp, he went to radio school in Chicago. He was then assigned to the battleship USS Missouri.** He had never seen a ship or an ocean until he arrived in San Francisco to embark. It was December 1944, about nine months out of boot camp, when he officially became a part of the Pacific war effort.

** USS Missouri History https://en.wikipedia.org/wiki/USS_Missouri_%28BB-63%29

CHAPTER TWO

Connecting to World War II

*"If something comes to life in others because of you,
then you have made an approach toward immortality."*
Norman Cousins

The USS Missouri was the last battleship to be built for
World War II. The Mighty Mo, as it was affectionately
called, was commissioned in June 1944. It was assigned to
the Pacific Theater of the war and was involved in two major
battles in Iwo Jima and Okinawa, as well as the shelling of the
Japanese islands.

My father's job aboard ship was in the radio room,
better known as the radio shack. It was full of transmitters
and receivers. Dominating the shack were rows of manual
typewriters. Several guys, including my dad, sat at those
typewriters wearing earphones and listening to the Morse
code. They recorded from Pearl Harbor, Guam, Headquarters
of the Pacific, or a flagship of the task force. The messages

Bob aboard USS Missouri

were typed up and given to a decoding officer. Less than a year after my dad boarded the USS Missouri, the ship was the site of the Japanese Surrender Ceremonies, on September 2, 1945, officially ending World War II.*

My dad wrote a letter to his parents from the ship just after it was announced that the war was over in mid-August 1945. He stated, "We are all proud that we have been able to help win this war. Let us all hope that this will be the last time that a war has to be won. Many of our friends have died with that hope. That hope has carried us through many a grinding, grueling day. Let us pray that it carries those charged with formulating and preserving the peace to a successful accomplishment of their task."

USS Missouri

---

* Surrender Ceremony on USS Missouri http://www.youtube.com/watch?v=Yh57jkS0Vaw

In his own words, my dad described the historic Japanese Surrender day:

"It started out as a gray day, sort of cool. Ships everywhere and lots of small craft. Busy, busy. Plying to and from the ships. Battlewagons, Cruisers, Tin Cans, Supply Ships, Service Craft were everywhere. Must have been the biggest assembly of ships ever. Lots of war planes too. Heavy patrolling. Everyone on board was in awe of the scene. We were in Tokyo Bay, at anchor, the first real port city since leaving Pearl Harbor in December. All guns manned, but you knew it was over. The defeat was complete. It was hard to believe what we heard about the big bombs.

"I wondered what it was like back home. What did they think; how did they feel? The whole world was focused on one ship, one event. We were it. It was hard to believe.

"Dignitaries and aides by the dozens started coming on board. All by water taxi as we were carefully at anchor, almost the middle of this huge bay. The hum of the hundreds on board and the constant roar of warplanes could be heard. Never before and never again. It was excitement, excitement. Heavy-duty thrill.

"Then MacArthur set the tone, very somber guy. Hollywood casting could not have matched his role, his presence, and his words. Born and bred for destiny and history. I really thought it was something to be there. The sun broke out as if on cue. A day to remember."

Like most veterans of that era, my dad didn't talk much about World War II. He had a picture of the USS Missouri in his home office, but not too much else around his house signified his participation in that war. I first saw his ship at the age of eight, when it was docked in Washington State at the Puget Sound Naval Shipyard. We had a family trip in the area and were able to go on deck and take some pictures. But I was too young to really appreciate the magnitude of the war or the ship's history. I wouldn't hear much about it or even ask him to tell me stories about his experiences until I was close to forty years old.

Lisa and Dad on USS Missouri

In my teens, I went through a phase when I read about the horrors of the Holocaust and the European part of the war. I did a short exchange program when I was sixteen that involved spending a month in Berlin, Germany. I saw the post-war aftermath of the Berlin Wall that divided the German people within their own city and country. I heard stories and saw memorials for those who died during their attempted escapes from East Berlin to West Berlin. I witnessed firsthand a city ravaged by severe bombing and the rebuilding effort that was taking place to restore it.

When I was in my late twenties, I visited the beaches of Normandy in France. I was incredibly moved as I gazed at the beach where the invasion took place on June 6, 1944, commonly known as D-Day. Seeing over 9,000 white marble headstones of American soldiers in a nearby cemetery who died that day haunted me. I visited the local museums that

Visiting ship 2005-Lisa and daughters

described the invasion and felt somber and humbled by the magnitude of the effort to free Europe and end the war.

It wasn't until after I divorced in 1999 that I started to go to Hawaii regularly with my dad. My daughters and I started to take trips to the islands each February, when my girls had a midwinter break from school. My dad often joined us. Whenever we were in Honolulu, we visited my dad's ship. It had been relocated there in 1998 and was made into a memorial and museum. Because the Japanese signed the surrender documents on the deck of the ship, the USS Missouri was retired and anchored in Pearl Harbor near the sunken USS Arizona.

On one of our trips to Honolulu, we visited the memorial of the USS Arizona. As we gazed at the water and the outline of the sunken ship below us, my dad could hardly speak and was visibly teary-eyed when he shared the story of how the Japanese attacked Pearl Harbor on December 7, 1941 and sunk the USS Arizona, entombing 1,177 officers and crewmen. The U.S. entered World War II and President Roosevelt declared it "a date which will live in infamy." That pivotal day saw over 300 Japanese planes bomb the U.S. naval fleet stationed at Pearl Harbor. Eight U.S. battleships were damaged and four were sunk. Many other smaller vessels were destroyed as well as aircraft. Thousands of lives were lost that day.

The United States raised or repaired all ships except the USS Arizona. They left the USS Arizona where it had gone down as the final resting place and memorial for all the men who had been below deck and entombed when it sank. By joining the USS Missouri with the USS Arizona in Pearl Harbor, the two ships represented bookends for the beginning and end of the war.

Whenever we had the opportunity to visit my dad's ship with him, it was an honor. He would then tell us more about his job as a radioman. The staff of the ship would give us a private tour below deck, especially to the rooms used for radio operations. Dad would relay stories about what took place, such as the time the ship was hit by a Kamikaze** on April 11, 1945. My dad was below deck at his battle station when the Kamikaze hit the ship, but he immediately knew what had happened and was concerned about casualties and damage. Fortunately, the Kamikaze had not succeeded in his mission to destroy the USS Missouri, since there was only minor damage to a 40 mm gun barrel. A lot of smoke went into a ventilation intake, but no one on the ship got hurt and there was no significant damage to the vessel.

The next day military rites were afforded the Kamikaze pilot as he was committed to the sea in a canvas bag with a Marine firing squad doing the traditional honors. The dent where the plane struck the ship is still visible today—I know right where to find it each time I visit. The crew was very lucky. Numbers vary, but up to forty-seven ships were reported as sunk by Kamikazes. Between April 1 and April 12, 1945, four battleships were hit by Kamikazes, for a total of 212 casualties.

** A Kamikaze was a small plane from Japan with a suicide mission to hit and destroy warships.

My dad, my girls, and I all attended the sixtieth anniversary of the surrender ceremonies on September 2, 2005. It was a very special event, and my dad enjoyed it. He loved being a part of something so important in our history and being able to partake in the ceremonies. The anniversary event was mostly a serious affair with lots of speeches, patriotic music, taps, flyovers, and military pageantry. But they also played music from the big band era afterwards, and it was fun to see my dad do the jitterbug with his girlfriend.

When the seventieth anniversary celebration was announced, I knew I wanted to go. But this time I would be representing my dad. He was in a rehab facility and not able to travel. I took one of his sailor hats and his radioman insignia, which I pinned to my dress. I was saddened to see that only about a half-dozen World War II veterans were able to make the trip this time, and I was told only a few others, in addition to that group, were still alive.

Meanwhile, back home my dad was actually interviewed on TV to talk about the day, and I was in text communication with a woman from the TV station, sending her live pictures from my phone of the event so she could include them in her coverage. He was sad that he was not able to attend the festivities, and it was a bittersweet honor for me to represent him. I know it meant

Lisa at 70th Anniversary
of End of War

a lot to my dad that I went in his place to honor him. He died less than two months after that day.

The whole experience of being with him on tours of the ship over the years has endeared me to the USS Missouri. I maintain his USS Missouri membership and hope to attend future anniversary events and celebrations. I know my daughters also have fond memories of our trips with him to the ship and will forever hold a special place for it in their hearts as well.

I am now the keeper of my dad's navy uniforms, pictures, and memorabilia from his service days. As a daughter of what many call the "Greatest Generation," the term made popular by Tom Brokaw when referring to those who grew up during the Depression and went on to fight in World War II, I am grateful for my dad's service and the ultimate sacrifice that many of his generation made to maintain freedom for our country and for the world. But as a daughter of one of this generation who survived the war, I also feel a responsibility to remember the other fathers and that era, sharing with my own children the lessons and history of that time.

If my dad had died of his first major heart attack in 1992 or any of the subsequent heart attacks and strokes he miraculously survived, it's quite possible that I would not have learned as much or felt the connection to his ship and World War II as I do now. Perhaps he hung on, living long enough to show, teach, and impart some of the story and the rich history to me. It is an honor to carry the torch as best I can.***

*** Japanese Sign Final Surrender https://www.youtube.com/embed/vcnH_kF1zXc

CHAPTER THREE

After the War

*"To leave the world a bit better, whether by a
healthy child, a garden patch, or a redeemed social
condition; to know that even one life has breathed
easier because you lived – that is to have succeeded."*
Ralph Waldo Emerson

When my dad was discharged from the navy in the summer of 1946, he returned home to Wessington Springs. He found that all the girls his age had gone off to college or married. He noticed two teenagers hanging out at the local swimming pool and thought they were cute, sweet, and fun to talk to but too young to date. One of those girls was Norma Jean Schwabauer.

President Roosevelt had signed the GI Bill into law, providing many benefits to returning veterans. One of those benefits was cash payment to cover college tuition. My dad chose the University of Wisconsin to utilize the GI Bill and left at the end of the summer to begin school in Madison.

His college plans were interrupted when his dad, Ralph, was hospitalized in mid-winter 1947-48. My dad left college at the end of the first semester and returned to Wessington Springs to help his mom run the hardware store. At the time, young Norma Schwabauer was attending high school and working part-time for a dentist, whose office was a half-block from the store. My dad started giving her a ride home. Driving around was all there was to do in a small town, but as a result of those car rides, their romance began.

Wedding Reception 1948

My dad and his parents decided to have a dispersal sale and sell the hardware business in 1948. Dad was then able to return to school, and he wanted Norma to go with him. Their folks were shocked because Norma was only sixteen. The couple eloped and married in nearby Luverne, Minnesota, on July 3, 1948. Upon their return to Wessington Springs, their parents threw a reception for them in the basement of the Methodist church. There was a big turnout—almost everybody in town showed up.

My mom, Norma, was the youngest child of a big family of eight. Originally raised on a nearby farm, the family moved to Wessington Springs in 1943. After the wedding, she accompanied my dad back to Madison, where she finished her senior year of high school as a married student. She then started taking classes at the university until children interrupted that direction.

They had their first child in 1950. My dad graduated in 1951, and he then moved west with my mom and my oldest brother. He'd researched nearby states that offered economic opportunities for new businesses coupled with a good climate and chose Colorado. Three more children were added to the family—a daughter in 1952, another son in 1953, and me in 1963.

While my mom stayed home and dedicated herself to raising kids and keeping house, my dad started his insurance career in Denver. Together my parents raised their four children in suburban Denver. As baby boomer kids, we grew up in the fifties, sixties, and seventies in the midst of a very traditional family life with a working father and stay-at-home mother.

In 1955, my dad founded and became president of The High Country Corporation, which specialized in surplus lines and high-risk casualty and property insurances. He worked long hours in that post-war energized economy, with a strong work ethic and a zest for success. His insurance firm prospered. His most notable client was motorcycle stuntman Evil Knievel. In the 1970s, he began to dabble in ranching

Businessman Years

Cowboy Years

and cattle on his weekends and decided to sell his insurance business in 1979.

Cattle ranching became his second career. He searched many areas to settle into his second phase of life and eventually found and purchased Prairie Canyon Ranch in 1980. Located in Douglas County, within arm's reach of Denver and seven miles south of Franktown, it seemed perfect for his "retirement" into ranching. He raised Texas Longhorns and later Red Angus cattle. Gone were the suits and professional attire he'd always worn in the insurance business. Now, he wore cowboy hats and boots and embraced this new look and life with gusto.

CHAPTER FOUR

My Birth and Childhood

"My family is my strength and my weakness."
Aishwarya Rai Bachchan

I was born at 8:26 p.m. on Saturday, February 23, 1963. My sister tells me that Mom and Dad went to see the movie, *Mutiny on the Bounty*, that day. I share my birth year with Brad Pitt, Helen Hunt, Mike Myers, and Whitney Houston.

A lot of interesting things went on that year. Most notably, when I was in the crawling baby stage, President Kennedy was assassinated on November 22, 1963.

Baby Lisa

Rev. Dr. Martin Luther King Jr. gave his "I have a dream" speech that year, and The Beatles got their first U.S. hit with "I Wanna Hold Your Hand." The Four Seasons were popular with "Walk Like a Man." *Bonanza* was popular on TV and *Tom Jones* won best picture at the Academy Awards. Gasoline was twenty-nine cents per gallon and a U.S. postal stamp was five cents. Life expectancy was 69.7 years, rising significantly from 54.1 years when my dad was born.

I arrived as the fourth and last child to my parents. I was a bit of a late baby boomer, born in the second to last year of that generation. Because my next oldest sibling was ten years older than me, and my two brothers and one sister were clustered together, born between 1950 and 1953, I often felt like an only child. By the time I turned eight, my siblings were out of the house and moving on with their lives.

I grew up in suburban Denver. It was a part of town with two-and-a-half-acre lots, so it felt open and uncrowded. I was loved and nurtured and had freedom to set off on my bike and ride anywhere I chose. There was no cell phone communication or helicopter parenting. Kids could go off and do what they wanted outside and then come back in time for meals or nightfall. For the most part, I was a happy, carefree child.

Dad with Little Lisa

My dad was a busy businessman and my mom a stay-at-home housewife. She made fabulous meals, and we rarely went out to dinner. I rode the bus to and from school each weekday. Mom timed baking cookies so that I would smell them fresh out of the oven when I opened the door upon my arrival home from school.

There was always plenty to do to entertain myself. As a child, I spent a lot of time outside. I was independent and self-sufficient. In winter, I amused myself with a good book, played albums on my record player, or worked on a puzzle. I begged my parents for ski lessons, and when I was ten, they let me join the Eskimo Ski Club. Throughout the winter, there was a bus or train that traveled to Winter Park every Saturday. Since my family did not ski, I went skiing with a friend each weekend. I was on my own for a day on the mountain and loved the feeling of independence at such an early age.

When the weather permitted, I loved to fly a kite or take long bike rides at sunset and even taught myself how to landscape, trimming shrubs and transplanting and arranging volunteer trees that sprang up in our big yard. Healthy and full of life, I also enjoyed ballet classes and was on swim team in high school.

In the summertime, we often took car trips to visit relatives in South Dakota or places like Yellowstone National Park; Jackson Hole, Wyoming; Sun Valley, Idaho; or the mountains of Colorado. Our family didn't have air conditioning in our cars back then, so we had to roll down the windows to cool off. As a child who had to sit in the back seat, I got blown by the wind and heat that came through from each of my parents' open windows. To keep me from getting cranky after the long hours of uncomfortable summertime car rides, as well as the boredom and restlessness that set in, they promised me a swim in the motel pool at the end of the day's travel. I remember that I often was given the opportunity to choose the motel. They gave me a few options in the town where we would spend the night, and I always picked the one with the best pool. I loved the responsibility!

I sometimes went to my dad's office to spend time with him where he worked. I amused myself by making photocopies of my hands or face or recording my voice in his Dictaphone.

My dad took pride in his business and his success. Because he worked so hard and kept long hours, he was rarely a spectator at my activities, including my swim meets. I didn't particularly mind that he didn't attend, since neither of my parents frequented my outside activities. It was the norm at the time for parents to allow their kids to participate in sports on their own. They didn't need to oversee each practice, game, or meet. For that reason, I didn't feel anything was lacking and was thrilled to have a delicious meal waiting for me when I got home.

Dad called me Putzer as a kid. I do not recall the story behind that name. He used to address birthday cards and valentines to me using that nickname. The name didn't bother me because he used it in an endearing way. As I became a teenager and developed a teenage attitude, however, the nickname gradually faded away.

My dad's father, my grandfather Ralph, died before I was born. When I was young, I expressed curiosity about the grandfather I had only seen in pictures. As kids often do, I asked how he died. My parents told me that Ralph was diagnosed as manic-depressive, which is now usually referred to as bipolar disorder. He ended his life in 1959, four years before I was born. In my dad's words, "He touched my mother, kissed her on the top of her head, then went to the basement and placed the barrel of his shotgun against his chest and pulled the trigger."

Despite the dramatic end to Ralph's life, my dad said that his father contributed to his later career success by instilling in him some wise advice. He counseled my dad with statements such as, "You'll never get anyplace working for someone else," "Don't buy anything that you can't pay for," and "A deal isn't a good deal unless it is good for both parties."

My dad's mother, Jane, died in 1966 of a heart attack, when I was three years old. My dad said she used to say things like, "Tell me who you go with, and I'll tell you who you are." Dad told me that she was strong and influential in moral values, well-dressed and groomed, good-looking, and very neat. She was friendly if she liked you, and she was cool and reserved if she didn't. She was a strict, good Methodist, who looked down on sinners and sinning. She loved being involved with local philanthropic organizations. I was given the middle name Jane in honor of her.

I am extremely grateful for my upbringing. My biggest obstacle to my perfect childhood was when my parents' marriage began to disintegrate in 1973. My older siblings had moved out of the house and were on their own by then. I was around ten years old when it became obvious to me that there were difficulties between them. I sensed tension

Bob and Norma 1963

and strain when they talked to each other. I also began to see books on my mom's nightstand with titles that revolved around relationship problems.

Everything changed after one particular warm spring day. I was in our TV room engrossed in a western show that was one of my favorites. My parents came in and asked if they could talk to me. I begged them to let me finish watching my show first, and they acquiesced.

I knew something was up, because "having talks" was not something we did. When my TV program was over, with foreboding, I slowly walked to the deck where they were both sitting. I sat down and could tell by the look of their serious faces that this was not going to be something good. They informed me that they were going to separate and were also considering a divorce.

I was dumbfounded. I didn't know what to think. Unlike today, divorce wasn't common back then. I only knew of one friend who had divorced parents, and we never talked about her family situation, since her parents had divorced before I met her. None of my friends teased or criticized me, but because separation and divorce were so rare, I immediately felt different from my peers.

My dad then moved to a spare downstairs bedroom. A few months later, he moved out of the house and into an apartment. As I watched my dad's progression away from my mom and our life together, my anger towards him grew.

Over the next three years of separation before the divorce, I heard my mom cry a lot, and I would either go outside or turn up the volume of my radio to drown out the sounds of her pain. I had a close relationship with my mom, and seeing her so sad was really tough on me. At my young age, I had no idea what to do other than look at my dad as the cause of her suffering. The blame I projected onto him added to the growing rift between me and him.

I chose to live mostly with my mom during their separation and ultimate divorce. No judge or court told me where to spend my time, which I appreciated. I wanted to remain in the house I loved, and I wanted as little as possible to do with my dad. I rarely stayed with him overnight, unless he took me on an insurance business trip. I accepted the invitation to join him when I was enticed by an interesting location, such as Biloxi, Mississippi, or Acapulco, Mexico. To add to the appeal to join him, he would show me a brochure of the hotel pool.

In the seventies before he sold his business, he went to many insurance conventions. His vice president was a woman who usually accompanied my dad to these business-related conventions. I didn't like her, because I thought my mom should be with my dad instead of her. My dad seemed quite happy, though—the polar opposite to my mom's emotional state.

This woman had a son, who was three years younger than me. Just like me, he also had older siblings and there was a large age gap. We were both like only children, since our older siblings had been out of the house as we grew up. While my dad was busy in meetings all day and social mixers at night, her son and I were left with each other and the other convention kids to goof off in the hotel pool for hours on end or play in the elevators until we sensed we would be caught. I barely tolerated my dad's business colleague, but I liked the companionship of her son. He and I became almost brother and sister and I often referred to him as my stepbrother. His mom and my dad never did marry, but they spent our growing up time together and eventually moved in with one another. Despite my dad breaking off this relationship in the early 1980s, I remained friends with her son.

During the seventies and eighties after my parents' divorce, my adolescent mind thought my dad was mean for having left my mom, and I had a lot of bottled-up anger towards him. Whenever I saw families eating together at restaurants, I felt painfully different from them. I didn't know how to dissipate the anger I felt, so I stuffed it deep inside and avoided my dad, because seeing him often stirred up my resentment. To the best of my abilities, I pretended my life was the same by not alternating houses. Living full time with my mom, I focused on friends and school.

When my dad sold his insurance business in 1979 and moved into his second career as a cattle rancher, his change in lifestyle held no interest for me. He took me to the Denver Stock Show every January, and I disliked it. He took me to some cattle sales, which bored me. When I visited him at his ranch, he drove me through his herds in his pickup, and the only reason I tolerated going out on drives with him was that it was fun to ride in the open end of a pickup or on the tailgate dangling and swinging my legs as he drove.

In my youth, I was alarmed at times by my dad's intense personality. Sometimes he was unkind to waitresses in restaurants. I remember one occasion when his harsh words caused our waitress to cry and never return to our table. Sometimes, he directed verbal outbursts to his sons. I was never the target of his yelling frenzies until the last years of his life, but witnessing him verbally shout at my brothers was heart-wrenching. He may have been trying to correct some behavioral situation, stop their back talk, or point out another type of mistake he felt they'd made, but I could never put my finger on the cause when it happened. Watching him yell at someone caused me agony and was another reason I avoided spending much time with him when I was young.

After graduating from high school in 1981, I went to a small college in Iowa for two years. This decision provided me with an opportunity to explore a new state and allowed me to be farther away from my dad. Homesickness for the state of Colorado, my mom, and my friends eventually brought me back home and to the University of Colorado. I had decided to major in physical therapy and was accepted into the university's program. I graduated in 1985.

My relationship with my dad was rarely on my mind at that time, and I kept distant from him until my late twenties when we had the first sign of his mortality.

CHAPTER FIVE

The Decision to Have Children

*"The first and greatest gift we can bestow on our
children is to be a good example."*
Sir Charles Morell

While attending the University of Colorado, I met my
future husband. I was twenty, and he was my first love.
My mom had gotten married at the age of sixteen, and she
had instilled in me the importance of completing college and
learning how to take care of myself by establishing a career
before marriage. I took her suggestion, and after graduation,
I worked several years as a physical therapist before I got
married in 1988 at the age of twenty-five. I continued working
in the early years of my marriage.

My dad was a healthy man without any significant ailments
until his late sixties. In 1992, I was twenty-nine, married for
several years, and working full time. While treating a patient
one day, the head therapist interrupted my treatment and told

me I had an important phone call. This was highly unusual, so I immediately knew something was wrong. After exiting the treatment room, she told me it was my brother and that he was calling about my dad. I felt my face drain of color as I walked to the office area to take the call.

My brother let me know that my dad was having a heart attack and was en route to a hospital in Denver. He explained that they had been horseback riding on my dad's ranch. My dad told him that he felt something was wrong—he had pain in his left arm and a heavy sensation in his chest. He said he had been feeling it for a few hours but it wasn't going away. He thought he might need medical help. So my brother had called the ambulance and my dad was being taken to the hospital.

I left work after finding other therapists to cover my schedule for the rest of the day. When I arrived at the hospital, the diagnosis of a heart attack was confirmed. My dad survived it and was able to go home within a few days.

Prior to this event, my dad and I had continued a strained relationship. I had never resolved my anger and blame towards him for my parents' divorce or my mom's heartache that I'd witnessed. From what I observed, he seemed to be living life like a man having a midlife crisis. Since their divorce in 1977, he was living wild and fast, moving from relationship to relationship, doing lots of traveling, and to me he seemed self-absorbed and arrogant. His behavior repulsed me, so I didn't see him frequently. But this near-death experience shook us both up.

His irritating qualities mellowed following the heart attack. The event seemed to humble him, and it became easier to be in his presence. He started to call me more frequently and invited me to do things with him. He suddenly and dramatically shifted focus to better his family relationships. I made the decision to meet him from the other direction and put more time and energy into doing things with him as well. I began to appreciate him more, realizing that I had almost lost him. It was a successful wakeup call for us both.

Within a month or two following his heart attack, I told my husband that I wanted to start having children. Emotionally, I shared with him that I couldn't bear the idea of my kids not knowing their grandfather. In acknowledging that he was, in fact, a remarkable man, I wanted our future children to know him personally, not just through stories and photographs. I had never met my paternal grandfather and couldn't remember my paternal grandmother. On my mom's side, her parents both died when I was fourteen, and I didn't know them well before they passed. I didn't want that to be my children's experience of their grandparents. I felt that my dad might have another heart attack, so the sooner we brought our children into the world, the more likely they would have the opportunity to have a relationship with him and remember him as they grew older.

My husband agreed, and I became pregnant with our first child a few months later. Our first daughter was born in 1993, approximately a year after my dad's first heart attack. Our second daughter was born the next year in 1994. My dad was excited about their arrivals and came to see them within hours of their births. He visited us often in those early years and was at every birthday and holiday party. He loved giving them presents and seeing them as often as he was able.

Most young children love to visit wide-open spaces where they can explore. Add a few farm animals, such as cows,

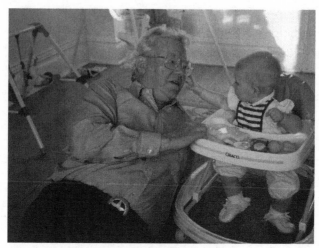

Grandpa and baby Summer

horses, goats, turkeys, dogs, and occasional kittens found in a barn, and my little girls loved to visit their grandpa and his ranch. My dad would take the time to show them all the animals, which sometimes included a brand new calf, and how to pet them while being safe. He then turned the girls loose and let them spend hours outside. Meanwhile, he created fabulous meals of chicken, potatoes, cornbread, and beans. When the meal was ready, he would ring a large bell to signal to them that it was time to come and eat.

As my little girls grew bigger, they learned to drive on his ranch. Starting when they were about nine or ten, I would let them sit in my lap and turn the steering wheel as we drove off the highway for a mile or so to his home. Then, as they grew taller, around age twelve and thirteen, I would spread my knees and allow them to sit on the seat so they could reach and push the gas pedal and brake themselves. By the time they approached fourteen and fifteen, I moved to the passenger seat and gave them full control. As they neared sixteen, I encouraged them to start up my car and take it from his house to the highway and back a few times while I visited with my dad. Dad and I watched from the dining room window to make sure they didn't drive off the road and into the creek.

We visited my dad at his ranch in all seasons and for many holidays. Those post-heart attack years were filled with special memories and a progressively closer family. With time, my mom and dad also began to talk more frequently, including occasional chats on the phone about family matters. As more grandchildren were introduced into the mix of family gatherings, they sometimes united despite their divorce. Gradually, my dad welcomed my mom to Christmas meals at the ranch and my mom would reciprocate by including him at some celebrations at her house. If I hosted a birthday party for my girls, I invited both my parents. They were polite and courteous in each other's presence.

My anger from the divorce years gradually softened, and I became more attentive to my dad and appreciative of his involvement with my family and the experiences he was providing my daughters as they grew up. He loved to expose them to ranch life, believing he was balancing their city upbringing. He expressed genuine interest in our lives by visiting us or calling regularly. Dining out and traveling with him became more enjoyable, too, as he modeled good manners and complimented waiters, receptionists, and other service and hospitality professionals. He seemed to grow kinder and gentler with age. I was grateful for the bonus time we had with my dad as a result of him surviving the heart attack.

CHAPTER SIX

Slowing Down

*"Resolve to be tender with the young, compassionate with
the aged, sympathetic with the striving, tolerant with the
weak, and forgiving with the wrong. Sometime in your life,
you will have been all of these."*
Lloyd Shearer

In the mid to late 1990s, my dad and I were busy with our
own lives. Recovered from his first heart attack, he resumed
flying to his favorite locations, such as San Diego and
Vancouver, or took road trips to South Dakota and nearby
states. He loved hosting or visiting his friends, dining out,
horseback riding, and collecting western or American Indian
items. He voraciously read magazines, newspapers, and
books centered on politics or history.

My husband and I were simultaneously absorbed in raising
our two little girls. They were busy with school and activities,
and our days were full. I was vaguely aware during this
decade that my dad was slowing down. I remember hearing
that his back and knees hurt following horseback rides.

Previously, he had taken weeklong rides with the Round Up Riders of the Rockies. I recall him saying that he had to give up this annual tradition because of pain. He began seeking chiropractic adjustments, massage, and physical therapy for various orthopedic issues.

When one of his knees became too tender to sustain his weight as he walked, my dad elected to have knee replacement surgery. Complications developed as a result of the procedure. My dad was resistant to moving his knee after the surgery in order to avoid feeling any pain. Yet, without daily and aggressive range of motion exercises, scar tissue developed, which caused him more pain and stiffness in his knee. I visited him at his home when I heard he was not doing well after he was discharged from the hospital. Despite my own profession as a physical therapist, I was unable to assist or persuade him to move his knee. He returned to his doctor and had to undergo forced flexion of his knee under anesthesia to break the adhesions that had developed. He was eventually happy with his ability to walk without pain, once he progressed beyond this post-surgical issue, but the experience made him shy away from having a subsequent knee replacement on the other side.

Gradually, he gave up horseback riding altogether and used his Argo or pickup truck to see the land that he had once viewed from his horse. As he became less mobile, his muscles and spine stiffened. He had difficulty turning his head to look over his shoulder while driving, and it was hard for him to stand up straight. I often suggested stretching exercises, but he did not embrace them. He did, however, enjoy and engage in water aerobics class at the nearby recreational center. I was thankful for that one form of movement that provided him a few hours of exercise each week.

Gradually, he had difficulty with car trips due to sciatica or neck pain. His knee that had not been repaired grew tender as well. He started to use a cane to take weight off his painful knee. He also started taking pain pills daily. Due to his dislike for exercise, I watched helplessly as he grew weaker despite the water exercise classes. The only reason he continued pool therapy was because the buoyancy of the water took the weight off his joints and lessened his discomfort. He also enjoyed the social aspect of the class and had met his girlfriend in the group. He respected my profession as a physical therapist but disliked doing any movement that caused him pain. I grew ever more exasperated with his attitude, but because I was busy with my young family, I shrugged my shoulders and resumed my focus on my own life.

In the late 1990s, my marriage was failing. In 1999, I divorced and had to begin to navigate the world as a single mom. The divorce had been traumatic, and I struggled for many years to recover and establish a new life for myself. My dad's aches, pains, and attitudes seemed trivial to me compared to the personal upheaval I experienced during my divorce. When my dad had another heart attack that required immediate triple bypass surgery while he was vacationing in San Diego in 2000, I was relieved that my brothers went to California to assist him.

Gradually, I rebounded from the divorce and my dad recovered from yet another significant heart event. We both began to travel again—often with each other. Since I was now taking my girls on trips as a single mom, my dad started to join us occasionally, which helped me feel less alone. We went to Hawaii, San Diego, and South Dakota multiple times during the early 2000s. While on the trips, he had to walk slowly, due to knee and back pain or shortness of breath. He took naps and retired to bed early. He began to ask me to drive when we rented a car and often we took the shuttle carts at airports to shorten his walk down the concourses.

As he aged through the 2000s, he switched from a cane to a walker. I watched with sadness as his posture continued to decline and he began to walk with a hunched back as he used his walker. Stairs became obstacles that he avoided. His trips became less frequent and shorter in duration. He took more and more prescription medication for his pain and his heart issues.

My dad never remarried after his divorce from my mom. He didn't seem to want to be alone, though, and was almost always in a relationship. He was an independent man but loved to dine and travel with a girlfriend. His last relationship was with a woman who lived near his ranch. Throughout my dad's eighties, they spent a considerable amount of time with one another. They seemed to fit well together and enjoyed many trips, celebrations, meals, and ordinary daily activities together. They were companions in their twilight years, always there for each other.

Her steady presence in the last decade of his life was instrumental in giving him the opportunity to stay in his home as his health continued to decline. When my dad grew less mobile after his stroke at the age of eighty-four, she stepped up her time and care of him. I was a busy mom, and I considered her an angel for being such a caring companion in his life. Her dedicated attention to his needs provided me the ability to focus more on raising my daughters and rebuilding my life following my divorce.

In his eighties, he began to experience some mini-strokes, one requiring a short hospitalization. He had a carotid artery procedure as a result of that episode and more medication was added to his daily routine. At this point in his life, I began to marvel at his toughness and resiliency to survive these events that were often fatal to others. Despite his aversion to pain and dislike for exercise, he puttered on. Looking back at those years of increasing fragility and decline, I think both my dad and I were in avoidance and denial about the reality of what was happening. We instead gave a sigh of relief that he had dodged another bullet and carried on. Neither one of us seemed willing or able to have tough conversations that might have been helpful to prepare for future disability and options to deal with potential issues, such as where he might live when he could no longer walk.

I mourned slowly as our rituals changed over the last three years of his life. My dad and I used to go to lunch together every Tuesday, and he would drive himself to the town of Castle Rock and meet me at a restaurant. We shared an hour of conversation over food and then went our separate ways. As he began to slow down, the drive seemed too much for him, and so I picked up lunch and brought it to his house. At first, he was appreciative of this gesture and always liked what I brought and thanked me for it. We talked at his dining table as we looked out the window at his beautiful view of the pond and meadow on his ranch. We adjusted to the new routine.

Over time on my Tuesday visits, I brought different food options and sometimes made him my homemade ice cream. Gradually, he began to complain about what I brought. He'd take a few bites and then would state that he'd had enough. Nothing I picked seemed to make him happy anymore. He told me the shrimp weren't big enough, the soup was better at another restaurant, or the sauce was too spicy. He demanded milk of a particular brand after every meal, and he questioned me during each visit to make sure I got the right kind. What had once been a meal we enjoyed together became an obligation and usually ended in me feeling like nothing I did could please him anymore. Sometimes he would thank me and sometimes he didn't.

In the last years of his life, I watched as my dad went from being well-dressed at restaurants, with a suit jacket and crisp, clean shirt, to wearing a grubby t-shirt and sweatpants with protective underwear underneath. I watched as his food dripped onto his shirt, and I often had to mention that he needed to wipe his chin when food collected there that he didn't seem to notice. He began to get progressively depressed and often teared up during my visits. Nothing I said seemed to console him.

In contrast, while my dad began to slow down in his final years, I felt like I was revving up in the prime of my life. In 2012, I sold my Denver house and moved to Breckenridge. My youngest daughter had graduated from high school that year. I wanted to downsize and simplify my living situation and finances.

I had been maintaining two homes until that point. My Breckenridge home was smaller and would have fewer expenses connected with living in it. Now an empty nester with my girls in college, I felt exhilarated with more freedom to travel. I embarked on this change in my home base with excitement to meet new friends and try new activities. I began to ski more, took country-western dance lessons, and became involved with various groups and organizations. I embraced and thoroughly enjoyed myself in my new town.

As my dad's mobility decreased, his world continued to shrink, and he relied on family and friends to come and see him. Seeing others lifted his spirits and helped to offset his depression, so I dedicated myself to driving to see him once a week despite the increased distance between our homes.

Although I was living a dream in my new life in the mountains, it was difficult for me to enter into a situation on a weekly basis that was the opposite of my happy state of mind. As I bounced back and forth between witnessing the ever-diminishing physical and mental state of my once-vibrant dad and my energized life in Breckenridge, I was painfully aware of the ongoing challenge it presented.

Additionally, despite the fact that my girls were in college, they still wanted my presence in their lives. They often came to stay with me in the summertime, during vacations, or on weekends. The daily demands of motherhood shifted since they were mostly at school, but they still desired my advice, attention, and time. As my dad's health deteriorated, the worry of it sometimes spilled over into my interactions with my daughters. At times I felt distracted during our conversations or had a hard time shaking off the dreariness of my last visit with my dad. On occasion I had to cancel a trip to see one of my daughters because my dad had a health event that required me to attend to him instead. The tension of the juggling act grew.

My dad frequently asked about the girls, wanting to know when they would come to visit him. It was difficult for them to see their grandpa's decline. They cherished his homemade meals when they had come to see him before, but now he was so tired that he could only offer them some of the leftovers from whatever meals others had brought him. He had always taken them on ranch tours, and now he suggested they go out and walk around while he took a nap. Their visits gradually became less frequent, and I felt I needed to cover for them, saying how busy they were in college. I felt stretched between the needs of both generations, as well as my desire to live my own life. The inner tension continued to grow.

CHAPTER SEVEN

Milk and Hearing Aids

"If you could choose one characteristic that would get you through life, choose a sense of humor."
Jennifer James

Perhaps it is impossible to live into one's eighties and not have a few irritating quirks—those qualities that make others' eyes roll combined with a headshake. My dad had a passion for milk that stayed with him until the end. When he was younger, it was Coors beer, Pinot Noir (pronounced very distinctly), beef, fried chicken, and my homemade vanilla ice cream, to name a few. His doctor ordered no alcohol after his stroke when he was eighty-four, and gradually his interest in foods diminished due to his lack of appetite.

On my regular Tuesday visits, I had to pick up and deliver to him a gallon of milk at his request. Not just any milk; it had to be 2%, from a store that carried milk from a particular dairy he liked, which required me to drive a bit out of my way for the weekly milk pickup. If I ran out of time and picked up another brand of milk at a grocery store, I was lectured and reminded about what milk I was required to bring on my next visit.

Midway, or near the end of our lunch, Dad would announce that he was ready for his milk. I would then need to immediately get up and fetch it for him. It had to be poured to a certain height in the glass. Often, he needed a few refills before he was satisfied. Sometimes I felt like Edith in the TV show *All in the Family*, who had to run to the kitchen and get Archie his beer whenever the whim hit him and he demanded it.

Occasionally, I encouraged him to drink water. In response, he'd argue with me that drinking water was the same thing as drinking milk. I never won that argument and eventually gave up trying to convince him.

Ultimately, I stopped being concerned about whether he drank milk instead of water. If it gave him that much pleasure, then he could have it. I'm almost certain that he had a glass of milk the last day before his death. Initially, his particular milk demands irritated me, but over time I stopped fighting a losing battle, which lowered both my and my dad's frustration levels. It seemed easier to laugh to myself about his quirkiness than to attempt to prove a point.

Hearing aids were another issue that caused others and me consternation. My dad was hard of hearing. He got two hearing aids at some point in his eighties, which were very helpful for him to participate in conversations, or listen to TV, radio, or anyone who visited him. Over the years, however, they would occasionally vanish for long periods of time. Sometimes they were found in a pile of clothes or some other odd location.

When his hearing aids were missing, I had to virtually yell to communicate. Not everyone was willing to talk so loud, so I was often the interpreter who would repeat what was said at a volume he could hear. I found being the interpreter an exhausting responsibility. When I left after visiting with him, I sometimes forgot to resume talking softly again and would find myself continuing to talk loudly with someone who had normal hearing.

In his last years, one hearing aid was never found and the other one didn't seem to work well. Many of us in the family tried to convince him to get new hearing aids. We thought it would help him, especially in social gatherings where he could not hear the conversations around him and consequently felt left out and isolated. We had also heard that a lack of hearing can worsen depression, which my dad continued to struggle with.

When I broached the conversation about getting new hearing aids, he refused, saying they were too expensive. Although he could well afford them, he said it was ridiculous to charge that much. He stated that he didn't want to perpetuate a scam by getting new ones. I soon realized that the hearing aid argument was just as futile as the "milk is the same as water" line of thought. I just had to accept that I would be fetching milk and yelling to communicate with him until the end.

CHAPTER EIGHT

The Final Years

*"Old age may seem a long way off. But on the day it doesn't,
it will be too late to do anything about it."*
Unknown Source

My dad moved from a stage of decline to disability when he suffered a stroke at age eighty-four in August 2010. His girlfriend called me from the hospital where she had taken him. They had been together at his dining room table one morning looking at the newspaper when she discovered he was having difficulty reading it. He also started to jumble his words as he spoke to her.

My girls were in high school and my youngest had started her soccer season. I recall visiting him at the hospital over the course of about three days, in between practices and games and getting the girls to and from school. The area of his brain most affected impacted my dad's cognitive abilities more than his physical condition. He had short-term memory problems, and it took months for him to regain the ability to read. He was able to return to his home to recuperate since he had maintained the ability to walk.

The following month, he had planned to attend a ceremony to induct Eagle Woman (1820-1888) into the South Dakota Hall of Fame. He had been instrumental in her nomination. He had read her history and believed she needed more recognition for her accomplishments, most especially her efforts for peace between her people and white settlers. She spent her youth with her Sioux tribe and also learned about the ways of white men, because her first and second husbands were fur traders. She understood the great changes the American Indians were facing as more settlers moved into the region. Eagle Woman often negotiated for peace between the whites and her native people, and my dad admired her diplomatic talents. So he wrote to the Hall of Fame in his home state and suggested she be nominated. As a result of his prompting, she was indeed inducted. Due to the stroke, he no longer felt able to travel. He reconciled his disappointment of having to miss the ceremony knowing that Eagle Woman's descendants were present to receive the honor.

He did not sustain observable paralysis and appeared to have been spared the often devastating changes in mobility that can occur from a stroke. However, the stroke had been significant, and his vitality and functional independence plummeted as a result of it. He needed more assistance with housework, laundry, meal preparation, keeping his medicines in order, and dealing with his mail and bills. Since he had never remarried after his divorce with my mom, he was accustomed to being self-reliant. His increased need for help coupled with his diminished independence caused him to feel more depressed. He relied heavily on his calendar and his girlfriend to remember things, to take him to appointments, and to keep him company and provide emotional support.

I watched my dad progressively experience loss of what he most loved in those final years. The stroke made reading a challenge for him. Driving his truck became increasingly difficult and unsafe. When my daughter's car engine died, he let her drive his vehicle, which was a blessing in disguise because it kept him off the roads. His progressive hearing loss made it more and more difficult for him to be a part of conversations. He wanted to visit my brothers in South Dakota one more time, but he decided he was not strong enough for such a long trip. He gave up wine, beer, and caffeinated coffee. He had been famous for putting together a fabulous Sunday meal of chicken or steak, mashed potatoes, corn bread, and baked beans, but he became too tired to act as chef. Some days, he stayed in bed due to extreme fatigue and depression. I watched as his world grew smaller and smaller.

In his last year of life, his inability to deal with incoming mail and his diminishing ability to read created the need for my sister and me to manage his bills, accounts, and correspondence. My sister was particularly adept at keeping his finances straight and would give regular updates to my brothers and me. We worked together as a team to ensure that nothing of major consequence slipped through the cracks, risking his savings and assets.

As I witnessed one of the most charismatic men I had ever met spiral downward, I mourned the loss of his strength, vigor, and independence. This slow unraveling of his life over several years often took the wind out of my sails for days after my visits. Gradually, I would regain my energy and enthusiasm for life during my days at home in Breckenridge. Yet, every week when the next Tuesday rolled around, the cycle would begin again. It was a sad time for us both.

CHAPTER NINE

Precarious Position

*"Avoiding danger is no safer in the long run than outright
exposure. The fearful are caught as often as the bold."*
Helen Keller

After my dad's stroke occurred, in addition to multiple heart attacks, I finally began to acknowledge how risky it was for him to continue to live alone. His rural ranch was south of Franktown, Colorado, approximately 30 miles from the southern suburbs of Denver and 120 miles from my home in Breckenridge. Weather depending, the drive from Breckenridge took me close to three hours.

My sister often visited on the weekend from her home, about 75 miles away from my dad's house. His girlfriend lived the closest, about a half-hour away, so she was the one who saw him most frequently. She brought him groceries and meals and kept him company in his isolated location.

His balance had been compromised from the most recent stroke and, as a result, he had taken a few falls. One time, he toppled over when he had bent down to pet a kitty. Thankfully, he only sustained a black eye and a sore back. Another time, I found him after he had fallen. I arrived with lunch on a Tuesday to find him lying on his porch. Despite a bloody gash above his eye, he was fully conscious and surprisingly calm. It turned out that he had been lying there for at least an hour. He'd gone out to look at his bird feeders when he lost his balance. He tried to get up but was not strong enough to lift himself, so he waited patiently for me to arrive. He had left his cell phone charging on the kitchen counter, so he could not call for help.

I am fit, but it took me about twenty minutes to figure out how to lift him. I tried all sorts of props and positions before we found a solution. We were both exhausted by the time we made our way back inside the house. I cleaned up his face and examined him. Thankfully, I only found bruises on his arms. Fortunately, it was summertime; otherwise, he might have frozen to death waiting for me to arrive. After these falls, we subscribed to a service and he began to wear an alert necklace. This gave us some peace of mind, although the device would not prevent a fall.

Taking into account his living situation, I had to acknowledge that his house was not in close proximity to neighbors or family and it was not built to accommodate his increasing disabilities. The reality was that he lived by himself and he was becoming weaker with each assault of illness or surgery. It was time to consider other living options for him.

It is a large responsibility to choose where a parent will conclude their life. It was a job I did not want to take on, but I was there and it needed to be done. His girlfriend offered for him to come and live at her house so she could take care of him there, but he declined her suggestion. My dad fiercely resisted the idea of moving out of his home. And who could blame him? It had an amazing view of open ranch land and Pike's Peak in the background. He could see a pond he had created and the geese that came each year to nest on the pond's island. He had daily visits from raccoons that he fed food scraps. He adored the birds that visited his feeders. He loved his two kitties that kept him company when he was alone. Dad was close to nature and its beauty, even when his progressive weakness made it hard for him to walk. He had a remarkable view from every window.

The inside of his home was equally inspiring. Surrounding him in every direction within the interior of his home was a plethora of artifacts. He collected everything American Indian—pictures, stone implements, arrowheads, drums, books, rugs, and authentic clothing. He also had an assortment of books, cowboy memorabilia from his days as a rancher, mounted buffalo, longhorn, antelope heads, and other historic collections that created the atmosphere of a museum in his living room. His personal belongings were important to him, and he owned a lot of them.

Gradually in the years following the stroke, I tried to broach the subject of in-home professional caregivers or of the possibility for him to move to an assisted-living facility. I came with a list of benefits—less time alone, people to socialize with, help with activities of daily living, meds, meals, and more. He said he liked being alone and didn't want any of that help. He said his girlfriend, my sister, and I were enough. I got nowhere with my discussions, and they only seemed to make him agitated and more depressed.

Because he vetoed the idea of moving, I began to explore options of in-home care. On two separate occasions prior to his edict to remain at home, we did find someone willing to travel to his rural location and visit him a few days a week to provide caregiver relief and extra help and company. His girlfriend was in her late seventies and dealing with her own health issues, so it was becoming more difficult for her to keep up with the increasing needs of my dad as he declined. My sister and I felt stretched, too, and I thought that adding another person to our rotating visitation schedule would be helpful to all of us.

In June 2014, I found a woman willing to visit him several days a week for a few hours to prepare a meal or two, do light housekeeping, and take care of any errands he might have for her. I arranged for her to come to the house to meet him and discuss the idea. The event touched a hot button for my dad. He was so upset that he created a scene when she arrived and we cancelled her employment before it even began. He then released an onslaught of anger at me. Never before had I been a target of his rage, and I dissolved into tears. The stress of the event and the subsequent strain in our relationship triggered some scary health problems for me. I spent several months afterward recovering.

Despite the severe reaction to our first attempt to get assistance and keep my dad at home, we tried once more to arrange additional help the following year. We found an agency willing to travel to his rural location to provide light care that we thought might fill the gaps between visits from his girlfriend, my sister, and me. At first my dad said he would try to remain open, but that quickly changed. He found something wrong with each woman from the agency who came to see him. At one point, he verbally snapped at one, which caused her to cry and leave, so we cancelled the service.

On several occasions, I suggested that we hire live-in help. I thought this idea would honor his wish to remain in his home and alleviate the weight of concern the three of us had for his safety and care when we were not able to be there. Unfortunately, he didn't want someone he did not know well to stay in his home. My dad seemed unable to acknowledge the emotional and physical toll his increased needs placed upon us. He insisted he could take care of himself, but the reality proved otherwise. He did not like leftovers or the plates of food left ready to microwave, so he let food spoil in his refrigerator and felt too tired to fix himself any meals other than cold cereal. The situation got to the point that unless one of us came to his house and put a plate of freshly cooked, nutritious food in front of him, he barely ate anything other than cereal or a nutritional drink.

In his last year at home, his growing weakness, coupled with emotional mornings when depression overwhelmed him, sometimes kept him in bed until after lunch, unless one of us came out to help him get going in the morning. The circumstances progressed to the point that he needed someone to be present and ensure that he was safe when he showered. He began to have difficulties with incontinence and soiling his bed, which required sheet changes. He sometimes forgot altogether to take his medication. At other times, he took his morning meds in the afternoon when one of us arrived to assist him.

The two failures in hiring caregivers left me feeling heavy with worry. His health was declining steadily as well as his abilities to care for himself. I no longer felt I could broach the subject of employing assistance or having him move away from his home. Our relationship was precarious. When I visited him, I felt challenged to identify what conversation would be calming to him. It often seemed that if I broached the wrong subject, it was a trigger for him and amplified his irritation, which left our time together strained. I floundered for what to do or say that would be helpful.

During this challenging time, a well-meaning friend suggested that perhaps my dad needed to be forcefully moved out of his house to a care facility. I laughed. Whatever relationship repair and healing we had experienced in our lives together would have been destroyed with that step. I was not willing to consider it.

His girlfriend, my sister and I resigned ourselves to continue visits without additional help. We knew that eventually something would happen to change it all. And it was almost a relief when it finally did.

On the afternoon before his fall and hip fracture in late July 2015, he had spent several hours sitting on his deck with a friend, enjoying conversation and his great view. Upon reentering his house, he turned in his kitchen and collapsed to the floor. He was not able to get up or move because of severe hip pain. It was obvious to his friend that he had broken it. My dad later claimed that he thought it had broken while he was standing, which then caused him to fall, but we will never know for sure. His friend kept him as comfortable as possible while they waited for the ambulance. My dad said that he suspected he would never see his home again. Sadly, it turned out that he was right.

CHAPTER TEN

Dementia, Drugs and Post-Surgery

*"Those with dementia are still people and they still have
stories and they still have character and they're all individuals
and they're all unique. And they just need to be interacted
with on a human level."*
Carey Mulligan

The roller coaster of dementia, drugs, side effects, and anesthesia recovery was enough to make my dad's caregivers and me crazy. And what almost made me lose my mind was the haphazard way these diagnoses and drug reactions were communicated and dealt with by the doctors and nurses who took care of my dad.

I knew my dad did not have Alzheimer's disease. But a week after his hip fracture, and shortly after his arrival at a rehab center, I was told my dad had severe dementia. Severe? I questioned who had made such a proclamation. I had to rewind from the chaos of the previous week and his hospitalization to figure it out.

When I arrived at the hospital the day after my dad's fall and hip fracture, I found a very lucid man, albeit a trifle loud as he yelled out in pain when anyone tried to move him or touch his left leg. He was clear-headed—he knew exactly where he was and what was going on. If no one touched him, he was amicable, and the nurses loved his wit and character.

He had to wait a few days before his hip surgery could be performed in order to allow time for the blood thinners he took for his heart to clear out of his body. On one of those waiting days, I ordered his lunch room service and suggested we share it. He liked the idea and said we would have a picnic on his bed. We did just that, sharing an egg salad sandwich and potato chips followed by a brownie. He told me I would always remember our little picnic, and I surely have. It was the last time I really remember us enjoying a meal together.

Everything changed after the surgery was done to place pins in his hip to stabilize his fracture. He told me he had no desire for food and that none of it tasted good to him. Everyone ordered from room service or brought in all the foods he had liked previously, but his taste buds couldn't get the knack of sensing those favorites anymore. To be fair, his enjoyment of food and his ability to eat a full meal had been waning significantly before his fall, but it took a deeper plunge after surgery. This change was disheartening to him and us because he missed the enjoyment and pleasure he'd once derived from food and shared meals. It appeared that the picnic we shared before surgery would be the last satisfying meal he could taste.

The elderly can experience negative reactions to anesthesia, including a loss of interest in food. My cousins, rather than my dad's doctors, let me know that this could happen and warned me that there might be other issues as well. In fact, my dad had many significant post-surgery reactions related to anesthesia. Not only did food not taste good to him, but he also had bouts of confusion, anxiety, hallucinations, delirium, and severe agitation. Prior to surgery, the nursing staff told me that my dad was their favorite patient. The story changed after surgery as the nurses became increasingly unable to deal with him. Two days before discharge to a nearby rehab center, a nurse gave him a drug called Ativan, which took all of the previously mentioned negative side effects and escalated them. The nurse immediately started to defend herself when I asked why my dad had gotten so much worse overnight. She later told me that she had given it to him to calm him down, stating that no one had told her not to give it to him. To my knowledge, he had never before had the drug, and a doctor conceded that it sometimes causes adverse reactions in the elderly. Ativan did not calm my dad down but instead made everything worse. By the end of the week, the nurses just wanted to get him off their floor.

For days after this incident, I approached every new nurse or doctor I saw and confirmed that Ativan would not be administered ever again. My nerves were frayed, and I was fanatical in my attempts to ensure that he not be given that drug or any derivative of it.

Gradually he improved, but it was a rough time for everyone during those initial weeks after surgery. When I walked into his room for visits, I wasn't sure if he would be clear-minded or irrational. And even in the middle of a conversation, he could switch instantly between the two extremes.

I felt blindsided with my dad's unexpected personality and mental changes. His hospital doctors were in a fix-it mode;

they minimized and brushed over the risks, side effects, and aftermath that sometimes occur for an elderly person after surgery. It felt to me that the family, nurses, and techs were left to clean up the aftermath. My dad had a successful surgical procedure, but neither he nor our family was adequately prepared for the rough road ahead.

CHAPTER ELEVEN

Rehabilitation

"Be nice to your kids. They'll choose your nursing home."
Anonymous

While awaiting surgery to repair the fracture and during the days that followed in recovery, it was obvious that my dad would need to go to a rehabilitation facility next. In our family discussions, we knew he would not be able to manage living in his home again. Besides the fact that his house was situated in a remote location, there were stairs he needed to climb to get inside the house and stairs to get to his bedroom. Together with his aversion to live-in or visiting help, the circumstances made it impossible to safely consider his return to his beloved home.

Dad had become so weak prior to the fall that I felt he was fast approaching the time when he would be an invalid in bed. In fact, sometimes he was only out of bed for a few hours during a twenty-four-hour period. On one of my visits in the month prior to his fall, I arrived at 2:00 p.m. for a late lunch, and he had not yet gotten out of bed for the day.

While my dad was in the hospital, I spoke with a social worker who provided the names and addresses of four nearby rehabilitation centers for us to check out. His girlfriend and I spent an afternoon touring them. We crossed off two shortly after we walked through their front doors. The look and feel immediately repulsed us, leaving us with the vision of a bleak parking lot filled with discarded people awaiting the end of their lives. Two others were new, looked bright, and smelled okay, so we took complete tours of their facilities. The residents seemed to be living and improving and the staff was working hard to give them a chance to go home once more.

Since I knew my dad was unlikely to return home, I chose the facility that had a skilled nursing floor where he could be transferred after the allotted time for rehabilitation had expired. The location was closer to his girlfriend's home, which allowed her to continue daily visits with Dad. In several spots in the hallways, I saw pictures of saddles, horses, dogs, and other animals, which I thought my dad would appreciate.

My dad's transition from the hospital to the rehab facility can only be described as a nightmare. He was in pain and experiencing almost every negative side effect one can have from anesthesia or medication. He yelled like a crazy man as they wheeled him out of the hospital and into the awaiting ambulance. I followed in my car on the ten-minute drive to the rehab facility. I parked and walked up to the ambulance just as they opened the doors to bring him out. He was delirious and still yelling. The ambulance crew told me that it had been one of the worst drives they had ever experienced with a patient. They were visibly shaken.

I put my hand on my dad's chest, leaned in, and told him it was okay. I kept trying to reassure him, but it was to no avail as we moved into the entrance of the facility. My calming words changed to a plea to stop his incoherent yelling. I thought he would scare all the residents as his stretcher was wheeled through the halls to his room on the rehab wing. Getting him out of the stretcher and into bed while releasing his arm restraints helped bring the hollering under control. It is difficult to put into words the gripping agony of that move. My dad's confused post-surgical mind took him to a place of fear that was irrational and extreme. I felt helpless to comfort or calm him.

When my dad's mental status had not improved much in the days following his admission to rehab, I asked a doctor what was going on. As I remember, he explained to me that anesthesia can settle into fat tissue of the elderly and then slowly release over the following four to six weeks as it gradually leaves the body. When it suddenly releases, the patient can show abnormal behavior and cognition. I braced myself for some unpleasant weeks ahead.

This same doctor told me that my dad had severe dementia, and as a result, he was not fit to make medical decisions for himself. Therefore I, as the designated medical power of attorney, was now in charge of signing all papers and making all decisions for him. The doctor's flippancy as he proclaimed my dad's dementia diagnosis felt dehumanizing to me. When my dad was rude to a therapist, I suspected they recorded him in their notes as a difficult patient. These attitudes bothered me, and my perception told me that my dad was now viewed as a crazy patient with dementia instead of the intelligent man I knew him to be.

In his first weeks after admission to the new facility, I fought for his dignity when he was unable to do it for himself by telling nurses, doctors, and therapists that he was not himself, that the Ativan and anesthesia had changed him, and that he was normally smart, pleasant, funny, and nice. When he was unpleasant, I begged them to be patient with him until he returned to his old self. In desperation to help him with staff rapport, I brought a photo album I had recently created and shared it with the caregivers who attended to him, showing them the person he had been years before ravages of advanced age had overtaken him. I hoped to remind them *and me* that he was still more than the pitiful old man with the label of dementia.

As my dad settled into his rehab after surgery, my once-a-week visits for lunch on Tuesdays extended to three days a week—Mondays, Tuesdays, and Wednesdays. I then had four days at home to recover. On weeks of surgeries or setbacks, I added more time to be with him. Each visit felt like an emotional roller coaster. When I walked into his room each Monday, I never knew if he would be clear-headed or irrational. I did not know if it would be a good day or a bad one.

When he first arrived at the rehab center, he was critical about the facility and the staff. He demanded I call one of his friends to come and see the terrible place he was in and do something about it. Then he told me to call his cardiologist and discuss what facility he would place his mother in if she broke her hip. He spit out these directives to me repetitively and with intense anger. On the other hand, if it was a pleasant day, he greeted me warmly and spoke to me kindly. He could oscillate between extremes within an hour. Sometimes during amicable conversation, he suddenly launched into complaints, telling me how awful the food tasted, that he didn't like a weekend therapist, or that he had too much pain and that medications were not being given when he needed them. Some of his protests were legitimate, and I ran around the center attempting to address them as best I could. Other issues were out of my control due to my inability to change the kitchen menu or staffing, along with the reality that he was one of many on a floor where almost every patient had pain or needed assistance.

During my visits, I sometimes had to leave his room and walk around the halls after he lashed out at me in frustration. His angry words cut into my sensitive heart. On one of my coping walks, I ran into my dad's physical therapist. Seeing my eyes brimming over with tears, he gave me a hug. Dad's occupational therapist was also supportive and did his best to let me know they cared.

For the first month in rehab, I had to remind myself that he was still under the influence of Ativan and anesthesia. Sadly, because I was the one who picked the place, he blamed me for what he considered a bad decision. It seemed that I became his scapegoat for the reality he found himself in.

Gradually, with time and the counsel of friends, Dad was reassured of my choice. Weeks later, he told me that he knew I had picked a good place for him. But the ordeal of making the decision, signing the paperwork, getting him transferred from the hospital, and his initial backlash had taken a toll on me. I had shifted from his daughter to a person who had imprisoned him in an institution against his will. I had signed the papers without him having the opportunity to read them first. Because he was deemed mentally incompetent after surgery, I was given all of the documents and decisions. But I couldn't tell him that; I just did what I had to do. It would have been a blow to his fragile pride and ego if I had told him that he could no longer judge for himself what was best.

On his good days and when the weather was nice, I took my dad outside and pushed him around the building in his wheelchair. Occasionally, he looked about, but most of the time he stared straight ahead. He was withdrawing, and the view of the parking lot didn't appeal to him. However, at times there was no denying that he still liked the sunshine, a light breeze of fresh air, and the spot where we could watch prairie dogs coming in and out of their holes. When we went on these outside excursions, he softened, but when we returned inside the building, his reality slapped him in the face. He was inching towards the close of his storied life.

During the course of his rehab program, my dad often said he needed goals. He would say that he wanted to go home, go on a drive, or visit a favorite restaurant. But when I had the occupational therapist practice a car transfer in and out of my car, he baulked at the attempt as being ridiculous, saying he would never be riding in a car again. He would sometimes work well with the therapist, yet some days he did not. He might give full effort to the exercise session, while at other times he would say that he was only doing an exercise to please the therapist instead of being able to acknowledge any value to him to progress towards his goals.

Because he now needed care around the clock, I could not realistically visualize my dad regaining the independent life he desired. Yet he would proclaim that he wanted to keep fighting. His emotions felt like a yoyo to me. For instance, although at times he said he was determined to improve, one day when he was feeling really down, he told me he wanted to die. When I relayed his comment to his doctor, he dismissed it and told me it didn't count because my dad had not said it to anyone else but me.

It was difficult for me to navigate the minefield of my dad's changing moods mixed with post-anesthesia confusion and episodes of dementia. I rarely felt I was making much progress in managing all his needs and complaints. It was a trying time for everyone.

His fall and hip fracture were a blessing and a curse all wrapped up in one. After admission to the hospital and then the rehabilitation center, he was not at home where he preferred to live and ultimately die, but he received around-the-clock professional care. He had a regular medication schedule, consistent oxygen, and was served three meals a day. I felt some relief knowing trained professionals attended to those items in a care facility. But the hip fracture was the beginning of a cascade of other health issues. Each time I walked into the building, it felt like I was fighting small brush fires with my dad's various complaints. Contain one and another ignites. Then the old one restarts and I'm running back and forth with a fire extinguisher.

Nurses were frequently different, and some knew how issues were being handled and others had no idea. A new nurse sometimes didn't know which fire was the focus. Some of my dad's issues were addressed and others were ignored or forgotten. My dad's complaints ran the gamut—from hip or back pain, difficulty sleeping, skin rashes and itchiness, leg swelling, the therapy schedule, the food, personality clashes with some staff members, the television stations, as well as a plethora of other important or trivial concerns. There was always a long list of issues—some coming from him and some coming from his girlfriend or other visitors. Prioritizing or solving any of them felt like a never-ending, hopeless job and created a sense that I could never sit down and just be with my dad.

His first room had a view of a courtyard, but my dad rarely looked out his window. He kept the blinds closed most of the time. His revered view was gone, and I suspect that looking out his new window only reminded him of its absence. He preferred looking at the walls or the TV screen when his eyes were open. He didn't even gaze at the framed photos of his family that I had placed on his nightstand and dresser.

At the time, I often wished that I could go back to the innocence of just being dad's little girl. As I grew older, he had evolved from calling me Putzer to Babe, but it was weeks before I got to hear the occasional "Hi Babe" when I came to visit. Mostly at first, he was mad and his anger had to be directed somewhere. That somewhere turned out to be me, the person who had placed him in a room without a view.

CHAPTER TWELVE

The Last Month

*"In the end, it's not the years in your life that count.
It's the life in your years."*
Abraham Lincoln

My dad's last month of life was October. I remember entering the facility and seeing signs of autumn and Halloween decorations adorning the entry and hallways. That month, he approached his three-month mark in the rehab program, his progress had plateaued, and his Medicare benefits were nearly depleted. The staff alerted me that we needed to make a decision about where he would go next. The therapists conceded that he could not go home. He needed continuous, around-the-clock care. The family had presumed this fact the moment he broke his hip, but initially the goal of rehab had been to return my dad to his house. After several months of daily observation, the staff and family finally reached the same page of understanding—he would not be going home.

I walked to the skilled nursing wing to make the arrangements for his transfer. I picked a sunny, south-facing room with a better view even if he didn't want to see it. I then handpicked some furniture from his house to give the room a homier feel. Over a weekend, I had a round table brought in with several chairs, so he and his guests could sit and visit or eat around it instead of my dad eating at a hospital-like tray table while his guests used their laps to balance their food.

I also placed a small rawhide in the center of the table and put pictures of people and things he loved throughout the room. I put a colorful blanket at the foot of his bed for him to use when he napped or to wrap around his shoulders if he got cold. I hung a painting his girlfriend had created of an old homestead with a grass roof that the two of them had visited together. I added a floor lamp and a bookshelf. Then I braced myself to give him the news of his impending move the following Monday. I told him that Medicare said it was time to switch rooms but that he could continue to receive therapy for a while longer. I did everything I could to make the news and the impending change easier for him to accept.

Dad, his girlfriend, and I, as well as his team of therapists and facility staff, all met in a conference room with a large table. Each member of his team gave a progress report and tried to put an optimistic spin on the upcoming transition. I stayed silent except to ask a few questions for clarity. My dad sat upright in his wheelchair, soaking it all in as best he could. When we left the meeting room, he asked to see the new room that I had chosen and prepared. I pushed him there for a look. He sat and didn't speak. I filled the silence with explanations of how I had picked the room and furnished it.

We then went to his old room and his girlfriend and I loaded his belongings onto a cart to make the room transfer. I scurried about and had everything put away in less than an hour in an attempt to calm my nervousness. After he was settled in, I departed. His girlfriend stayed there to keep him company while I assisted my brother with packing some of his treasures from his house to move to South Dakota. My dad wanted his cherished collectibles to move to my brother's house in South Dakota for safekeeping instead of being vulnerable to theft in an empty house. My brother had driven to Colorado for a visit and to help pack some of his prized possessions. He and I then planned to visit Dad the following day.

The next morning, I visited my dad after his first night in his new room. It was an unremarkable visit—he was calm and engaged in the normal routine of the facility. His girlfriend had called me the night before to tell me that she and my dad had noticed all the touches I had done with the room. She told me he appreciated it, but he seemed unable to express that sentiment directly to me at my visit. Late morning, I said goodbye in preparation to return to Breckenridge, knowing my brother would be spending time with Dad before he drove back to South Dakota. Hours later, I was preparing to leave Denver for home when my brother called me.

My dad had developed severe abdominal pain in the afternoon and was headed to the ER. I reversed my direction and headed there to join my brother, my dad's girlfriend, and my dad. While we waited hours for tests and the results, I sat and looked at his telemetry machine. It showed so much heart arrhythmia that its alarm was perpetually triggered. The staff stopped listening to it.

The verdict of gallstones was finally conveyed to us. We were told that he would require surgery. However, they would need to wait a few days to discontinue his blood thinner medication before they could proceed with the surgery. I left his room that night with a heavy heart. There would be more anesthesia side effects, more time in a hospital, and the inevitable lost strength from being bedridden.

I had no idea that he would never fully recover from the procedures and the complications that came from them. In retrospect, after everything played out, I realized how ironic it was that the day after his move, my dad had a sudden development of an internal crisis—one that would catapult him to the end of his life.

My dad spent less than two weeks in total in his new room and just under three months overall in the facility. I don't think he desired to live his life for long outside his own home. I have heard that some elderly people do adjust to a nursing home, but my dad never did. I suspect he decided he would rather die, and so he did.

CHAPTER THIRTEEN

The Last Three Days

"A man's dying is more the survivors' affair than his own."
Thomas Mann, *The Magic Mountain*

In the months after my dad fell and broke his hip in late July 2015, my routine changed to accommodate his needs. I spent three days in Denver, visiting him each day, then I returned to my home in Breckenridge for four days to rest, recover, and live a bit of my own life.

My dad's last week was on the same schedule. I needed the rest even more than in previous weeks, as I found myself so exhausted that I felt on the brink of collapse. For months, I had been living a roller coaster of emotions. Some days, my dad's condition had seemed so bad that he did not want to talk, eat, or get out of bed. Other days, he perked up and had a good day—engaging in conversation, participating in therapy, and going to the dining room to eat with other residents.

The unpredictable cycle of decline and rebounds caused my nerves to fray, and the weight of managing his care while visiting him in rehab created constant tension for me. There were always issues to be addressed, such as which medications to give him, which to discontinue, and what dosages to administer. Each day, he seemed to have varying symptoms, such as agitation, sleepiness, mental confusion, constipation, urgency, frequent bowel movements, skin itchiness, leg swelling, stomachaches, and pain. Each practitioner had different suggestions and sometimes those proposals clashed. Certain requests for things to be done were taken care of immediately and at other times they were ignored or forgotten.

His mood was as variable as his symptoms, and I received calls or emails from his girlfriend, other visitors, and my sister after each visit to assess what had happened that day and what could be done differently. Often, a morning visit would be a completely different story from an afternoon or evening visit. Because I was his medical decision maker, I received reports from staff and visitors and then had to decide how to deal with what was happening. I sometimes threw up my arms in exasperation and frustration.

By October, the pressure of handling his ever-changing status and care had even caused my low back to go out. I could hardly move. Although the condition of my back was very real, it was simultaneously symbolic. It was as though my back was telling me that it could not carry this heavy load of responsibility any longer.

On Wednesday in the last week of October, when I left Dad after a challenging visit, I sensed that it might not be a good idea to go home. I felt he was nearing the end and could die at any moment. However, because of his propensity to be tough and stubborn, as well as his capacity to surprise me by bouncing back, I had begun to doubt my ability to accurately gauge when his death might occur. I wondered if I should stay, but I was so exhausted that I longed for my home and my own bed. Our time together had been so stressful, due to his move to a new room, re-hospitalization, surgery, and resistance to my help, that I couldn't deny my need for a break. I craved rest more than ever and my back was still aching.

I emailed an update to my siblings that day:

Sent: *Wednesday, October 28, 2015 12:33 PM*
Subject: *Update*

Rehab doctor is officially saying Dad has pneumonia. He is being given antibiotics.

Yesterday I offered him the breathing device to exercise his lungs and he waved it off. Today I offered it and he became hostile and I thought he was going to throw it across the room. He told me to never give it to him again. He really only wants to lie down and rest.

When I come in and say hi, he knows who I am and will say hi back but that seems to be the extent of his desire to converse with me.

He is not much interested in therapy but I gather he does what they ask. He says he does a few things so they can mark it off in their notes that they did something. He seems to do it for them and not himself and I wouldn't be surprised if he refuses soon.

Dad had been glad to see me when in the hospital (and beforehand) and maybe a bit when he first got back to the rehab center after discharge from his gall bladder surgery, but my visits over the last 3 days are a different story. Polite, non-engaged indifference has now turned to irritation bordering on hostility. He doesn't look me in the eyes unless he is getting angry, then he glares at me.

With a heavy and weary heart, I did leave my dad late Wednesday morning to return home. To further muddle my mind, a friend called to tell me later that evening that he'd had a great visit. My dad had watched the presidential debates on TV and had been lively and interactive. I received such a good report that I was shocked. It was so different than my time with him that morning that I was speechless. I crawled into my bed Wednesday night feeling like I had no grasp of my dad's true condition.

When I awoke Thursday morning looking forward to a few days of respite, I heard my phone ringing. The screen displayed the name of the rehab center. I always dreaded those calls, particularly since I felt my dad was slipping. I answered, and the nurse told me that my dad was not doing well. He was experiencing chest pain, an irregular heart rate, and fluctuating blood pressure. They wanted to send him to the ER. I had just reviewed *Gone From My Sight: The Dying Experience*, written by Barbara Karnes, and I knew these symptoms might be his body approaching the end.

I calmly and bravely asked if the ambulance and ER would respect his "Do Not Resuscitate" directive. I did not want heroic acts done to keep his heart beating, such as chest compressions, defibrillation, intubation, respirators, IVs, or any other interventions that might make him suffer and prolong the death process. She responded that he did not have to go to the hospital and that they could attempt to make him comfortable. I told them to do that and wait to make the decision to send him to the hospital until my sister arrived. She was on her way to spend the day with him.

About an hour later, I got another call that he had stabilized and was no longer in any discomfort. His rhythms had come into more balance. My sister would stay the day and monitor his situation. She encouraged me to stay home and rest, so I did, but I had the nagging feeling that things were going downhill quickly.

My sister gave me a report later in the day that her visit had been good. She said she would return the next day and re-emphasized that I should stay home and recuperate. I still felt nagging conflict and guilt that I was at home and not there. I felt unsettled inside, but I chose to stay home as she had encouraged me to do.

On Friday morning, I got another call from the rehab center saying that my dad had the same symptoms as the morning before but worse. I told them to keep him there and that my sister would soon be arriving to assess the situation. Again, he stabilized and my sister said he was comfortable. She planned to spend another day with him and would do the same the following day. Again, she told me to stay home.

All day Friday I felt uneasy. I didn't want our last encounter, which seemed extremely negative to me, to be our final one. I felt I should go and see him and just hold his hand, allowing him to say anything he wanted or needed to say. But, because my sister was there, I had coverage for three days and felt we needed to take turns and separate our visits so each of us could refresh and replenish ourselves when the other was there. I reminded myself that I would see him on Sunday, a day earlier than my usual Monday visit, which was only two days away. I ultimately decided to stay home.

Later that Friday night, October 30, I was at an evening Halloween dance when I saw my phone ringing. My sister was calling. I had a habit of keeping my phone out so I wouldn't miss any calls. No matter what I was doing, I was always on edge—and on high alert. When I saw it was her, I had a sinking feeling and looked at my friends next to me at the table with weary and worried eyes. I picked up the phone, wondering if she was going to tell me that our dad had died. Instead, she gave me a glowing report of what a good day he'd had. He had even eaten a good supper, which was not always the case. His appetite had been dismal lately. She told me that she would be back to see him in the morning and just wanted to give me the good news. I was shocked and relieved. I told my friends the great news and was finally able to relax a bit with them and enjoy the rest of the evening.

Saturday morning arrived. It was going to be my third day of rest, and I knew I would see Dad again the next day. My sister's call the night before had been quite reassuring, and I now felt like I would see him the following day and all would be okay. About 9:00 a.m., the rehab center called again. I was becoming accustomed to these daily morning calls, since he seemed to have much more difficulty in the mornings. This pattern of challenging mornings had been happening for a few years and the last two mornings' calls represented amplified versions of this pattern.

Expecting to hear that his heartbeat was once again irregular, and his blood pressure erratic, I said hello. The nurse introduced herself and immediately cut to the chase. She told me my dad had died. She reported that he had chatted with the nurse at 6:00 a.m. and there had been no indication that anything might be wrong. There had been no cause for alarm or concern at that time. When someone went in at 7:00 a.m. to take his blood pressure, the attendant found him dead.

Whatever rest I had begun to feel from being home for a few days evaporated as a flood of different emotions set in. In those first moments after the call, I felt relief that his suffering was over and deep sadness that he was gone.

The day was filled with one emotional phone conversation after another as I notified the rest of our family and close friends of his passing. When it was time to go to bed, although I was exhausted, I could not sleep. Even sleep aides didn't help. It was a miserable night as I lay there feeling restless and unsettled. When I awoke the next morning—the day of my planned visit—I felt a gaping hole. I suddenly realized that I had missed the chance to say goodbye.

CHAPTER FOURTEEN

The Day After

"Death leaves a heartache no once can heal.
Love leaves a memory no one can steal."
-from a headstone in Ireland

I woke up exhausted from a fitful sleep the day after my dad died. I had tossed and turned the night away, only finding snippets of shallow slumber to relieve my overactive mind. I saw flashbacks of pivotal moments in the last three months of his life. I remembered the call I received that he had fallen in his kitchen when he broke his hip. Random scenes of the hospitalizations, surgeries, and rehab that followed his hip fracture wove in and out of my awareness. In my semi-sleep, my mind seemed to be piecing those events together and reconciling that his struggle was now over. At the same time, my thoughts went forward to all the tasks I would need to do now that he had passed.

As I stirred with the light of a new morning, I lay there thinking about the day ahead. This was supposed to be my day to visit my dad. It should have been my turn to spend a few days with him after my sister had stayed with him. I visualized sitting with him and holding his hand. In my mind's eye, I had hoped for a day of just being with him without directing him to do anything or managing his care. I wanted to have a day of being his daughter again instead of the conductor of his orchestra of treatment.

Suddenly, the scene in my mind switched to the reality of our last day together, four days prior. I wanted to change what I saw—the memories of what had actually transpired. I wanted to erase the image of the angry glare my dad gave me that last day and replace it with a softer expression. Because he had developed pneumonia, I had prompted him to do his breathing exercises. But he had only wanted to go to bed and rest. My logical mind told me that it was essential to clear his lungs with deep breathing.

Because the nurses and therapists had many patients to attend to in the facility, I often filled in the gaps for them by assisting in the suggested treatment for his care. As a result of my role of medical decision maker for my dad and my past career as a physical therapist, I rarely felt like I could just show up as a visitor. During his three months of inpatient care, my visits were busy with gathering status reports from nurses, therapists, and other medical professionals. I envied others who just walked in the door and simply sat with him. I wanted to have that kind of day to counter the unpleasant interaction we'd had when he became angry with me for suggesting the breathing exercises. Unfortunately, there was no way to change any of it. He was gone, and there was no possibility of rewriting our final moments together.

I sat up, and with a heavy heart, got out of bed, dressed, and gathered my clothes into my travel bag that I had used for my trips to Denver each week. I forced myself to eat a bit of breakfast and made some coffee to help with the fatigue from so little sleep the night before. After packing up my car, I headed out from Breckenridge for the two-hour drive to Denver. From there, I'd make my way to my dad's home near Franktown, another forty-five minutes southeast.

After a somber drive during which I continued to ruminate about the past few months and all that would need to be done now, I first stopped at the rehab center where my dad had passed away the previous morning. As I parked and passed through the entryway doors, I walked right by the sign-in desk. If the receptionist wanted to chase me down, so be it. I didn't feel like exchanging pleasantries or logging in my visit to an empty room. I rounded the corner and walked down a hallway full of doors to residents sitting in wheelchairs and recliners brought from their home or lying in their beds. Most residents seemed quiet that morning but I recall hearing one individual who was groaning.

Because the facility was primarily for rehabilitation, and most of the residents were staying there temporarily, I had watched several discharges. Family members came with balloons or flowers to take their mother or father to an awaiting car and home. Often there were grandchildren, too, and all were excited to be leaving. I knew when my dad was admitted that he was declining rapidly and was unlikely to leave alive. As I walked on towards his room, I felt a tinge of bitterness. The vehicle that had come to pick up my dad was a hearse and the destination was a mortuary. I didn't blame the place or the staff. It was just his time to die, yet I couldn't help but think about the "what if" scenarios.

Not wanting to engage in conversation with anyone, I purposely averted my eyes as I passed the nursing station. Thankfully, I didn't see any personnel I recognized. I continued down another hallway to the far end of his wing where patients resided who had not been able to go home after their rehabilitation phase was over. Like my dad, they were too sick or disabled to graduate from the facility and were essentially parked, waiting for their exit from this world.

When I got to my dad's room, the door was ajar. I pushed it open, walked in, and stood at the threshold. Only twenty-four hours earlier the room had been full of my dad's stuff and the smells that accompany the life of an eighty-nine-year-old man living in a confined space. On any other day before yesterday, I might have found him resting in bed or sitting in his wheelchair, with the television news channel droning on in the background. Now the room was quiet and smelled only of disinfectant. The bed was neatly made and finished off with the facility's standard mauve-colored spread. There was not a trace of my dad left anywhere.

I moved around the room and opened every closet and drawer. All were empty. Even his nametag had been stripped from the plastic holder beside his room number that had been displayed outside his door. The facility had immediately turned over the room in preparation for its next guest. From the sterile look and smell of the room, it was as if my dad had never resided there—as if he'd never even existed.

After a few minutes, I began to wonder if the last three months had all been a dream. I stood in the middle of the room and allowed myself to sense whether or not his spirit still lingered. I felt nothing. He was gone. From the very beginning of his admission, he'd made it clear that he didn't want to be there. Along with his body that had been removed the previous day, his spirit had gone as well. It hadn't stayed long enough to wait for my return.

I knew it was time to leave. Because it was a Sunday, my dad's regular therapists and nurses had the day off. I was rarely there on the weekend, so I didn't recognize the staff that day. I doubt I could have contained the sadness I held just below the surface if I'd made eye contact with a familiar face. I retraced my steps, purposely not looking at anyone as I went down the hallways for the last time.

The cool air that hit my face as the automatic sliding doors parted to let me out gave me slight relief from the disappointment that enveloped me. It wasn't the end of the story I wanted to remember. It was a sad conclusion to a grand life of nearly ninety years.

I had declined to drive down the previous day to view my dad's body before the mortuary picked him up. Visitations or viewings of the deceased had never appealed to me in the past. In my mind, his body was a shell. His soul had left, and I did not want to overlay the visual of a lifeless corpse with my memories of a once-vibrant man. I didn't want to hold a cold and stiff hand. I much preferred to remember his warm, soft hand as it gently squeezed mine.

Truth be told, the facility had not asked me to come in the day after his death. My sister and my dad's girlfriend had already removed his few personal belongings the previous day. I just felt compelled to visit his room one last time. Maybe it was because this should have been my day to see him, or maybe I wanted to feel if anything unseen might be lingering there. I was also seeking a bit of closure I had not been able to have with him before he died.

As I drove to my dad's home south of Franktown, I thought about the fact that he had last been there three months earlier. He had cherished his land, his house, and his view. As I exited the highway, entering Prairie Canyon Ranch, and drove down the single-lane dirt road, weaving past rolling hills and pastureland, I tried to breathe in the vistas and see it the way my dad would have if he were sitting in the passenger seat next to me. It was autumn and the hay had been cut and gathered in the field, which now lay in wait of winter snows. The green of an occasional ponderosa pine dotted the brown grassy hillside.

I drove over the creek, which was a slow trickle at this time of year. I glanced at the pond, but the Canadian geese had already left, migrating south for the winter. I drove through the farmyard that contained an old homestead, barn, chicken coop, machine shop, and garages. It was no longer the working cattle ranch it had been just a few years prior. My dad had sold the property to Douglas County Open Space fifteen years earlier. At the time of the sale, the ranch had a herd of red Angus cows, a few Longhorns, horses, goats, chickens, ranch dogs, and barn cats. A hired man and his wife had lived in the old homestead house and actively worked with the cattle and hay pasture. Gradually, the county had ceased to continue with the livestock operation, discontinuing the lease the hired couple had maintained for over a decade. For the last few years, all that remained were a few aging Longhorn steers and my dad's two black cats who decided to move from the barn into his house. The county allowed my dad to continue to live on the ranch in the house he had built on the hill overlooking the farmyard and pond.

I wound through and behind the buildings and made my way up to my dad's house on the hill. He had it built in the early 1980s with the help of my brother, who was a carpenter. I parked my car and grabbed the key that hung from a nail on the porch beam. Letting myself in, I knew the kitties would no longer come to greet me, since they had already been moved to a new home, his girlfriend's house. Dad's house was uninhabited except for a few houseflies. It was stuffy and the air stagnant from all the closed windows. I walked into the kitchen and dining room, which were noticeably tidier than when my dad lived there. His dining table had been stacked with mail, newspapers, magazines, books, and notes he had scribbled on pads of paper. Over the last three months, I had occasionally stopped by his house, retrieved his mail, and slowly sorted through the mess, attempting to organize the chaos of his workspace and ensure the bills were paid.

I walked on and went straight into his bedroom. The furnishings were unchanged, except that the bed was neatly made. I sat on his side of the bed, where four months earlier I might have found him napping when I came to visit. I picked up his wristwatch from his nightstand and looked at it. Then I started to talk to him. I told him I was sorry that I didn't have a chance to say goodbye. My shoulders started to quiver and the sobs came up from deep within. The pent-up sadness I had held contained while visiting the rehab center released. I am not sure how long I sat there as the tears flowed. Time seemed to slow. Whereas his nursing home room had been devoid of his presence, his bedroom seemed almost too small to contain his incredible spirit. It felt like he put his arm around me to comfort me. I told him that I loved him. His essence told me the same.

His hip fracture forced the departure from his home. My sister had foreseen this event, voicing the thought to me that due to his progressive weakness, he was on the brink of a fall. She also expressed that when he did fall, she did not visualize him returning home, because it was remotely located and poorly designed for someone of advanced age. Sadly, when my dad drafted the plans for building his new house while in his fifties, he did not seem to look to the future and anticipate the possibility of disability. There were stairs everywhere and bathroom doors were too narrow for a wheelchair to pass through.

Before his fall when I had contemplated my dad's death, I thought that due to an extensive cardiac history he would have another heart attack—a final fatal one. As it turned out, my sister and I were both correct. He did fall and his heart simply stopped beating.

As I sat on his bed, I felt certain he would have preferred to die there—not in the sterile institution he found himself in after his fall. But progressive decline and complications from surgeries necessitated a two-person maximum assist to get him in and out of bed as well as skilled nursing care in his final weeks.

After my tears had run dry, I returned to the kitchen and dining room and stood looking out the big window at the view he loved so passionately. Dusk was approaching and the light of the day was fading. There, beyond the ranch land, stood majestic Pike's Peak.

I could hear the hum of the refrigerator, the ticking of a clock, an occasional fly buzzing, and a thud as it hit against a window. Otherwise, all was still and quiet. It seemed as if everything reflected the remains of a glory day gone by.

Absent were the vibrant ranching operations and farm animals visible from the dining room window. Autumn encompassed the land, bringing with it the sense of an upcoming cold, snowy winter that waited just around the corner—the land going dormant just like my dad's house. This house that had once been filled with lively conversations, large family meals, and spirited holiday gatherings was now just a memory.

After a long pause and a big sigh, one last teardrop rolled down my cheek. I glanced at the living room, which was filled with furniture, collectables, and books. I tried not to think about the upcoming task of removing all of his stuff in the two months before year's end when the lease on his house would be up for renewal. The job of cleaning out the house was too heavy for me to dwell upon that day. Taking in the scene out the window once more, I turned and walked out the door as the sun was about to set.

CHAPTER FIFTEEN

Mourning

*"Life is not the way it's supposed to be, it's the way it is.
The way you cope with it is what makes the difference."*
Virginia Satir

There are two types of loss: sudden and gradual. Sometimes gradual aging provides time to adapt due to so many little losses along the way. Sometimes surviving into old age gives one a chance to grieve before death so that the end comes as almost a relief. And sometimes a gradual death gives one a chance to say goodbye. I say "sometimes," because it is not a guarantee that living to an advanced age or dying gradually will give one any of those opportunities, or that an individual will take advantage of any such opportunities.

In a way, my dad had both a gradual and sudden death combined. The family was not called to sit with him in his last days or hours. He died alone, speaking to a nurse within an hour of his death. I expected death, but not on that morning. And because I didn't see his death coming when it did, and planned to see him the following day, his death felt unexpected. Since my dad did not know or would not openly admit that he was dying, we missed the chance for those conversations that included a final "I love you" and "Goodbye."

Dad had not wanted a traditional funeral and was cremated. To honor our dad, our family planned to schedule two celebration-of-life events—one in Colorado on his beloved ranch and one in his hometown in South Dakota. Each event would have a private family gathering to spread his ashes. We decided to delay the celebration-of-life ceremonies to dates in the future when the weather would be warmer. The delay would also give us a chance to plan the event, gather addresses for invitations, sort through the photos from his long life to create a pictorial of a life well lived, and attend to all of the details for those traveling from afar. Thus, in the week following my dad's passing, I went on a trip.

I traveled to a beautiful beach that took my breath away. The water was a turquoise color; the sand was white and soft as powder. In the distance there were white fluffy clouds with deep blue sky surrounding them. The different hues of blue, green, and white were brilliant by day and other colors of orange and pink came as the sun set. I brought all my senses into each scene, as I listened to the waves hit the shore and crickets chirp in the grasses near my beach chair, tasted delicious conch salads and rum punches, and smelled the salty water mixed with suntan lotion. I loved the warm feel of the sun on my skin and the soft sand between my toes. All the surroundings brought my focus to beauty and helped calm my frazzled mind.

I found that the loss of my dad triggered the memory of another loss in my past. I lost my father in death, but years earlier I'd lost my husband in divorce. There were parallels in the two losses: my dad's health declined gradually and my marriage failed slowly. My dad died unexpectedly, and my husband told me about his plans to divorce suddenly. Both men were important male figures in my life. I found myself thinking more and more about the loss of my marriage after my dad died. I had to discern whether I needed additional closure from my divorce or if the loss of my dad just touched the same nerve.

As I mulled over important questions, I realized that grief and love are intertwined. Deep grief is not a weakness; rather it shows that I chose to love deeply. My former husband was my first love, and I gave him all of my heart. So, of course, I was devastated when he chose to leave our marriage. I do not regret having had the courage to love someone so fully. I gave him my entire heart without holding back. I was blessed with two incredible daughters from that love. After my dad's death, I acknowledged that depth of love and grief again. I allowed both losses to exist together.

My trip was one of the best things I did to shake myself up and out of my habits and constant doing of things that needed to be accomplished. I had a multitude of items that I needed to address upon my return, but the trip launched me into an awareness of my need to be mindful. While I was away, my pace slowed and I took time out to rest. When thoughts of sadness, guilt, or other emotions that did not feel good came to me, I allowed them to drift in and then out without entertaining them much. I practiced observing each thought without attachment. I simply looked out at the beauty around me and let the thought float by like a seagull drifting in the air above me.

In some ways the trip delayed my mourning. The moment the plane landed and I disembarked for a layover at the halfway point home, the tears came. My mind and body had needed a brief break, and I was grateful that I'd listened and took the trip. It reminded my mind and body that it was possible to rest and replenish. It gave me permission to allow healing and beauty back into my life. The incessant mind chatter quieted a bit on the trip. By breathing more, talking less, and taking in the scenery around me, I was able to get a grip on myself, which allowed me to return home, be with my emotions, and begin to deal with settling my dad's affairs.

CHAPTER SIXTEEN

The Dream

*"Six weeks after his death my father appeared to me in a dream...
It was an unforgettable experience, and it forced me
for the first time to think about life after death."*
Carl G. Jung

One night about two weeks after my dad died, I had a vivid dream. I walked into the hospital to see my dad. When I arrived at his room, he wasn't there. I asked the nurses where he was, and they told me he had been transferred to a place for rehabilitation. I became very upset. I stated that they weren't supposed to move him until I got there. They explained that they'd already moved him. I asked where they took him. They answered, "On 75th." I asked, "75th and what cross street?" They would not tell me. I became increasingly upset, shouting that they could not take him before I got there. I was agitated and distraught.

Then I looked around the room and he was suddenly there. I exclaimed, "You are still here!" I was surprised to see his condition. He looked at least ten years younger and was standing tall and upright. He was dressed in beige slacks, brown loafers, and a white dress shirt. A man I did not know was helping him put on his favorite orange corduroy jacket as the finishing touch to his outfit.

I walked over to him and he turned. I gave him a big, long hug. No words were exchanged. When I released him, he momentarily lost his balance and teetered a bit. I put my arms out to steady his swaying and he slowly came to balance. Then he was gone.

The dream shifted to another scene, and I was in the car of some man I did not know who promised to show me where they had taken my dad. But he was driving crazily, missing highway exits and swerving on the grassy shoulder of the road. The man would not tell me where we were going. When it became obvious to me that he was not going to take me to my dad, the dream abruptly ended.

I pondered the dream when I woke up from it in the middle of the night and in the days afterwards. My interpretation was that my dad had healed a lot since his death, because he could stand upright and was wearing nice clothes. He was still off balance, as his journey in the afterlife was still new and he was probably still trying to get his bearings. I believe I was angry in the dream, because they took him before I got to his room. In reality, he died the day before I planned to visit him. The man driving the car would not show me where he was, because it wasn't my time to go there.

Shortly after I experienced this dream, I cleaned out my dad's closet. I donated his clothes to the Salvation Army, but I kept the orange corduroy jacket. It reminds me of the vibrancy of his life. I could not change the timing of my dad's death. It simply was what it was. The dream did not feel like a dream—it felt incredibly real. Both the dream and my dad's jacket remind me that his spirit lives beyond his death. I'm forever grateful to have hugged my dad one last time, even if it was in a dream.

CHAPTER SEVENTEEN

Cleaning Out the House

"The more you get, the more you got to take care of."
Alice Dormann

When I returned from my brief reprieve, it was time to clear my dad's house. It was mid-November, and his lease would be up at the end of December. I did not want to extend the lease after my dad had died. With winter storms coming soon, it was time to empty his house.

The task felt heavy long before I started it. My dad had accumulated vast quantities of stuff in his home. Some of it was valuable and some of it was junk. I wished he had gotten rid of all the junk as he aged, but it just got shoved in the basement in piles.

My dad liked to collect things—especially Native American Indian, cowboy, and western paraphernalia. My oldest brother made multiple trips to haul those items to storage in South Dakota for the eventual integration into the new house my other brother was in the process of building. Since I had developed into the role of leader and organizer in most matters concerning my dad, the remaining contents of the house became my prime responsibility to sort, disperse, or dispose.

I was often alone for an afternoon amongst his belongings, and I was exasperated with the task of cleaning out a lifetime of accumulated stuff. As I filled bags for donation or trash, I had to curb my resentment. There were many treasures in his house, but there was also a profound abundance of items that I felt he should have discarded years before to lessen the work after his death. The weight of loss from his passing felt even more pronounced by the stress of clearing out his house.

Because there was so much to dispose of in a short period of time, I wasn't able to appreciate moments when I found something interesting along the way. I felt sad, because I sensed my dad would have wanted this final experience in his home to be more positive. I wrestled in my mind the conflict between the task at hand being a burden and a gift.

At times, I was able to find humor in the process, especially when I came across certain items he'd collected, such as toothpicks in plastic wrappers from restaurants. Each time he went to a restaurant, Dad would grab several toothpicks at the hostess stand and put them in his jacket pocket. I looked into the pockets of each item of clothing before I donated his clothes. Each pocket contained toothpicks.

As I cleaned out his desk, kitchen cabinets, and nightstand and bathroom drawers, each contained dozens of those plastic-wrapped toothpicks. I figured it was harmless to be a toothpick collector, and when I found them at every turn, I just had to laugh. I had no idea why he was worried about being without one, but it must have been a concern or a habit gone mad.

Each week until the end of the year, I spent time at my dad's house clearing it out room by room. The days of the week when I previously visited him were now spent packing and hauling the artifacts of his life to other places.

Emptying out his closet full of clothes and bathroom cabinets were the hardest for me emotionally. Discarding his personal toiletries made his departure from life more real. As I sorted his clothes, it stirred memories of events and times when he had last worn certain outfits. I kept the one orange jacket that he wore to most of our lunches—the one he'd worn in my dream. Initially, I found myself smelling it and smelling him. Eventually, I put it in a protective bag in my closet. Perhaps I will get it out in the future, but at the time I closed it up in a bag, the jacket had become too difficult for me to look at regularly. I also kept a few hats, cowboy boots, and scarves he always tucked into the breast pocket of his suit jackets. Keeping a few clothing items helped me to remember his days as a sharp dresser and think less about the food-stained t-shirt and sweatpants days of the more recent past.

My dad had numerous coats and over forty pairs of jeans, many with flannel insulation. When I scheduled the donation pickup, I wondered how many underprivileged or homeless men might have a warmer winter in Denver. He had quite a few fabulous suit jackets and ties as well. I also envisioned that men might be wearing these outfits to a job interview or to work.

I set a personal goal to have the house cleared by Christmas so I could rest the last week of December with my family and start the New Year with the house clearing complete. A few days before Christmas, I stood in his dining and living rooms and stared at the open space. Decades of living had disappeared, but the walls still showed a hint of the past from the discoloration where picture frames and animal head mountings had once hung. The only sound I heard was from the kitchen wall clock, which still ticked. No one in the family had wanted it. The clock seemed to fit the spot by the door perfectly and matched the wood molding of the room, so I left it behind. Time would continue to be marked by that clock in the house. It would remain the witness to the past and the future of that space and would continue ticking after I left the house keys on the counter and closed the door behind me for the last time.

After his death and the complete cleaning out of his house, I worked on the picture-sorting project. I placed the best pictures in photo albums that could be enjoyed at his celebration events and then remain as treasured mementos for our family to remember his long and amazing life. Seeing his nearly ninety years of life spread all over my dining table as I put together the albums helped me to see beyond the narrow focus of his last three years or his final three months. As I enlarged my vision to see the bigger picture of my dad's full life, I was better able to let go of getting stuck in memories of its end.

Ultimately, I created multiple albums, scrapbooks, and a slide show of over 700 photos. I knew if I didn't do it then, his photos would most likely never get organized or viewed by the younger generation of our family.

After his two celebration-of-life events took place, I printed pictures of the celebrations to place in the box of albums. I had purchased a sturdy, plastic container to store all the neatly created albums and scrapbooks. Nine months after his death, I finally felt I had sufficiently preserved his life pictorially. I mused that I had perhaps become addicted to the process or that my lack of resolution at his death had kept me going to the point of mild dysfunction. Maybe I was holding on to him with my projects. No matter the reasons, in my own way, in my own time, I was processing and letting go gradually in the year following his death. His house was empty, but the work within me was not yet complete.

CHAPTER EIGHTEEN

Coincidence

"Every so-called coincidence or answered prayer is God's way of giving you His small, silent communication. A little wink saying, 'Hey kid! I'm thinking of you...right now!'"
SQuire Rushnell

I have read about the departed making their presence known to those left behind. I have heard that God or the deceased can give a signal or provide a coincidence to send a message that the deceased is still with you in some dimension—out of sight but not far away. I have experienced coincidences before, but I had never personally experienced one connected to a departed loved one. I wasn't looking for such an event. I was simply proceeding with life after Dad's death.

Dad had always liked parties. He especially liked parties for major milestone birthdays. And I was the one in charge of organizing these birthday bashes. I had held one for his seventy-fifth, eightieth, and eighty-fifth birthdays. He would hint that he wanted these parties, and it was assumed that

I would make sure they happened. He died just shy of his ninetieth birthday by six weeks.

I knew Dad would have wanted a party even in ill health, and I was certain he wanted one dead too. So I found a Sunday just before his birthday in December and I rounded up family and close friends for the event. My dad loved the restaurant The Ship's Tavern, at the Brown Palace Hotel in downtown Denver. I had been there many times with him over the years. The reservation was set for noon. In attendance were my two daughters, my sister, my mom, my dad's girlfriend and her daughter, as well as two of my dad's friends.

We sat down and it was decided to bring up an empty chair at one end of the table opposite where I was sitting in honor of my dad. My dad's friend ordered the Warsteiner beer my dad liked and placed it in front of the empty chair along with a piece of Melba toast with butter on it. My dad had liked the Melba toast the restaurant served and would slather it with butter while he waited for his meal. Later, his friend drank the beer, but the Melba toast remained at his setting throughout the meal.

Before much time had passed at the beginning of the meal, we saw his naval ship, the USS Missouri, on the TVs scattered around the bar, signaling his presence to me. I nearly shouted at my daughters at the other end of the table to look at the TV. I thought they would know and feel what it meant. We looked at each other with knowing ... he was definitely there with us!

SQuire Rushnell, in his book *When GOD Winks at You*, says a godwink is a coincidence that seems to be a direct message of reassurance from God to you. Seeing my dad's naval ship on TV at the beginning of our gathering felt like a personal message to us. Rushnell says these godwinks are "delivered at just the right time to assure you that you were not alone—that Someone was up there watching over you in a very personal way."

We ordered a bottle of Pinot Noir for the table because that is the type of wine my dad preferred to drink when he wasn't enjoying a beer. We gave a toast to him to commence the meal. The lunch proceeded well and everyone seemed to enjoy themselves.

Towards the end of the meal, I alerted the waiter to give me the check. I had decided that I would use the last of my dad's cash from his wallet to pay for his birthday lunch. He was essentially treating everyone to this birthday meal, which he would have done if he were still alive. He'd had $374 in his wallet. I had no idea what the bill would be when I opened the black folder.

My dad always did a funny gesture once he saw the figure on the bill: he caused the bill to jump in his hands and acted shocked by the amount, so I did the very same thing to create a few laughs around the table. Then I looked at the total. It was $377.76 (just $3.76 from being exactly even)! I could not believe it. It was so perfect that I knew it had been orchestrated by him to make absolutely sure we all knew that the cash amount left in his wallet was purposeful and that we had spent it in just the way he would have wanted it to be used. Best of all, he was there with us, and he wanted to make sure we knew he did not miss his important birthday.

I had held myself together for the event, but I was emotional most of the rest of the day. I was deeply affected by what I felt was his communication to me that he was there with us. It was important to him to reach out to me and to anyone in attendance who was open to that possibility. Whether that was God or my dad's spirit, or a combination of the two, it didn't matter. As the afternoon and evening progressed, the serendipitous moments during the lunch hit me harder than I thought they would. As the day went on, it became evermore clear to me that my dad knew what we were doing, approved of our celebration, and was there with us. I was moved to tears by what happened, and I am incredibly grateful that he spoke to me.

My dad's friend wrote an email to me later that day. He had previously told me that earlier in the year he had brought my dad there with his girlfriend for lunch.

"I realized later today that the reason your Dad ate so much (ate the most I have ever seen him eat, crazy!) the last time he was at the Brown, was because he needed a reserve for today since he only got a piece of melba toast and an empty beer glass. Even though he was there today, he knew ahead of time that he would not be able to eat with us."

My dad never liked to miss a party, especially if it was in honor of him. I am glad he showed his presence and his approval. In reflection of the events of that day and the dream I had the month prior, I have remained open to the divine messages they might contain. Perhaps he came to say goodbye, and maybe he wanted us to know he was still with us but in another dimension. Considering both possibilities made me feel better.

CHAPTER NINETEEN

Unwinding and Revitalizing

*"There must be quite a few things a hot bath won't cure,
but I don't know of many of them."*
Sylvia Plath

I took a lot of baths as my dad's health declined. They did help. I knew I needed more than just baths to fully recover, but baths were definitely part of the process. It took me awhile to unwind from witnessing my dad's decline. Time needed to pass before I could view his whole life instead of just the suffering at the end.

A cousin told me that it took a while after her mother died before she could remember other memories instead of the grueling end of her life as she suffered with cancer. Each person has a beginning, middle, and end of life. My cousin told me that, in time, I would draw from more and more memories of pleasant times earlier in my dad's life. I looked forward to releasing the trauma of his last few years and welcomed other memories when they came to me. When a good memory surfaced, I let my mind linger on it and let unpleasant ones fade. I did not stifle hard memories, but I tried not to get enveloped by them. My dad's life was magnificent, but only if I let myself see and remember more than his years of decline.

Gradually I moved through time, the house was cleared, holidays passed, and affairs were getting settled. I felt the gradual return of more energy, but I still didn't feel peppy or experience a vitality that I had enjoyed in the past. I still wasn't myself. I attempted some form of exercise each day, sought my acupuncturist, and scheduled a massage. I read a few novels and humorous books. I ate healthy food and foods that I particularly liked. I listened to soothing as well as more upbeat music. I continued taking baths. I experimented with what might bring me a sense of vibrancy again. I found no particular key to bring it back, just a willingness to see what might work coupled with the desire to feel good again.

Unwinding from the trauma of my dad's last years, months, and days took time and occasional travel away from the immediacy of all the things that needed to be done. My revitalization is still an ongoing and conscious practice. I find patience is essential. I attempt to focus on what has gotten better instead of what still seems lacking or still troubles me. I affirmed that I would get through the period of mourning and put my life back in order, as well as find purpose and passion again. I dwell on gratitude for all I have and am because of him. I acknowledge the circle of life and do my best to carry on.

PART TWO

Reflections

*"No one wants to die. Even people who want to go to heaven
don't want to die to get there. And yet death is the destination
we all share. No one has ever escaped it.
And that is as it should be, because Death is very likely the single
best invention of Life. It is Life's change agent.
It clears out the old to make way for the new."*
Steve Jobs

CHAPTER TWENTY

Acknowledging the End of Life

"A life well lived deserves a good ending."
Angelo E. Volandes, M.D.

Angelo Volandes is a physician and researcher at Harvard Medical School. He admits that doctors often fail to communicate about how to live life's final chapter. "Without this open conversation about death, patients are traumatized needlessly, leaving their families with the emotional scars of witnessing the hyper-medicalized deaths of their loved ones."

A century ago, most people died at home with their family around them. Now, for a variety of reasons, many of the elderly die in hospitals, nursing homes, and other institutions, often surrounded by people they do not know. Dying alone in the skilled nursing wing of a rehab facility, the last person my dad saw before he passed was a nurse he barely knew by name. He wanted to be in his home, but he had become too weak and needed skilled nursing care around the clock. His final days oscillated between miserable and slightly tolerable. His well-lived life concluded in a nursing home environment, but mercifully for him, he lived in his beloved home until three months before his death.

I longed for my dad to initiate dialogue with me about his care while he still lived at home. He had experienced multiple heart attacks, which left his heart damaged and weak. He had also had several strokes, which also reduced his ability to function. He had fallen multiple times. He experienced increased frequencies of incontinence and diarrhea and no ability to clean himself or his bed after these incidents occurred. He needed assistance with almost every aspect of self-care and meal preparation. With ever mounting disability and dependency on others for help, I wished he would ask me questions about what options he had and what I would recommend.

Due to my background as a physical therapist, I knew that exercise might have helped his balance and muscle strength, creating more stability and mobility. But my dad disliked exercise and claimed he was too tired to do any basic movements with me when I visited him. I sometimes left him with a few written exercises on a piece of paper, such as pumping his feet up and down while he sat to increase circulation to his feet and relieve ankle swelling. But by the next week, the paper was buried in the ever-increasing piles of papers on his dining table.

My dad was a smart man and savvy in money matters. He studied investments, researched interest rates, and read about estate planning. Over ten years before his passing, he completed essential financial management steps to avoid probate and delineate the settling of his estate. He had even selected a mortuary and completed the paperwork for cremation. These documents were all in a box ready to be handed to me to execute upon his passing. Planning for his death from a business perspective was something he took seriously, and I appreciated his thorough preparation.

However, planning for his death from a personal perspective by managing his care and where to live felt like a taboo topic. In his last few years, as his weakness and fatigue increased and his mobility decreased, his emotions became fragile. When I came to visit, his eyes would often well up in tears. The cause of the tears varied. Sometimes he was sad after hearing that a friend had died, which was becoming ever more frequent in his later years. Other times he stared out the dining room window at his few remaining Longhorn steers. He had been accustomed to feeding them himself but was no longer physically capable. Often, his tears stemmed from his desire to return one last time to South Dakota to visit my brothers and see his ranch. Dad would express how much he wanted to go there and then admit he felt too weak to manage the trip. It was hard for me to know how to respond when he became despondent. It was heartbreaking for me to witness.

Despite his admission that he was increasingly tired, had many areas of pain in his body, and felt his muscles weakening, he didn't want to discuss that his body was failing. I sensed he wanted something outside of himself to alleviate his suffering. He seemed to cling to hope that there was another intervention that might help, such as a sleep apnea apparatus, an oxygen machine, or an adjustment of his medication. Despite lying in bed for many hours each night, he never felt rested in the mornings. He woke up depleted physically and emotionally.

I sensed that broaching the topic of end-of-life care would signal to him that I was giving up or that he should give up. He appeared closed to the reality of his situation—that he was no longer able to care for himself at home. Yet, privately I wondered if he knew more than he could or would express. A few times he actually said to me in low points of despair that he wanted to die. Sadly, those moments didn't lead to meaningful conversation because he became suddenly agitated, someone interrupted us, or he shut down when I prompted him to expand on what his comment meant. I was frustrated that the few times we came near to a very important point of honesty, it never fully progressed towards openness between us.

When my dad was admitted to rehab, his doctor told me that he was not able to understand the degree of his disability. He lacked mental clarity to see his needs, plan his day, and navigate safely from event to event. As a result, the facility, with its routine, therapists, and nursing staff, guided him. If left on his own, he would not have known what to do or when to do it. This doctor was adamant that I needed to make his decisions.

In retrospect, our family waited too long to talk about end-of-life issues together with our dad. At some point in the last three years before his death, my dad had reached a time when he was not capable of those conversations. In his later years, I simply thought my dad had a difficult personality, which had been my experience for most of his life. I did not know much about the ravages of dementia. I understood my dad did not have Alzheimer's disease. But he did have dementia, and the demented person can fool you. Because he knew my name and was generally lucid, I did not fully comprehend that he had lost perspective of his own care. The window of opportunity to plan and prepare for the end of his life had closed gradually. Any cracks left open to talk candidly were tenuous and fleeting.

I now urge friends and acquaintances to have conversations with their aging parents and within their families while their parents are still relatively healthy and of sound mind. Scenarios can be discussed with loved ones before emotions become fragile or mental capacity is compromised. Multiple contingencies can be mapped out and various solutions identified. The discussions have the potential to create basic roadmaps to guide both the parent and the family, yet allow for flexibility as life unfolds.

In the year prior to my dad's death, when he still lived at home and was progressively becoming weaker and losing the ability to care for himself, I felt in desperate need of help. I called his doctor's office and begged the nurse to talk to my dad's doctor to encourage looking at end-of-life issues and decisions with Dad at his next visit. I inquired about hospice services. Although his doctor's nurse was compassionate, she told me that my dad did not qualify for hospice. He appeared to them to be managing his life and his health relatively well. For instance, when I attended doctor appointments with him, my dad wore nice clothes and put up a good front that he was doing better than he actually was. If I interjected a few truths, such as his reluctance to exercise, and informed them that he had taken a few falls, my dad became upset. I felt myself in a sticky spot as a daughter and desperately needed a third party, such as a doctor, to address his declining function and end-of-life considerations of safety, comfort, and care management.

Often before visits to my dad's doctor, my dad's girlfriend would tell me that due to her own heart issues as well as fatigue from the ever-increasing needs and demands of my dad's care, she also wanted outside help for him. She spoke to me privately that she was at a breaking point of exhaustion and could not carry on much longer and maintain her own health. I had hoped that at doctor's visits she might chime in to mention her concerns. Yet she was often tentative and quiet, acting more as a support for dad than herself.

Admittedly, we both had experienced my dad's backlash after doctor's appointments. He fixated on something one of us said and would proceed to rant about it for what felt like hours. We both tried to change the subject to another topic, but he would circle back to his irritation again and again. We tried to explain ourselves and what our intention had been related to our concerns for his well-being, but neither logic, diversion, nor apologies calmed him down. He often remained in an agitated state after a doctor's appointment until he went to bed. When he awoke the next day, it seemed that the episode had been forgotten for him, but his girlfriend and I suffered ongoing anxiety and frustration as a result of those appointments.

In the February 2015 edition of *Minnesota Medicine*, Barry Baines, M.D., and Janelle Shearer, R.N., B.S.N., M.A., wrote an article entitled, "Let's Talk to Our Patients About Hospice." In their research they stated, "We found many doctors are willing to have a conversation about serious illnesses with patients and their families, assuming the patient initiates the conversation. At the same time, we found patients were waiting for their doctors to start the conversation and bring up hospice."

Barnes and Shearer continued in their article, "When we spoke with physicians, many said the biggest barrier to referring patients to hospice care was patients being in denial about their illness and/or not accepting that they have a serious condition. Patients may not fully understand their condition. Without this fundamental knowledge, they can't even begin to ask questions about options for their care."

My dad may have been in denial and he certainly had no personal experience dealing with aging parents. He had substantially outlived his folks by reaching the age of eighty-nine. His father died at age sixty-two, and his mother died suddenly of a heart attack at age seventy-one. He never had to consider or manage their end-of-life care. My mother had elderly parents who passed while living in a nursing home in South Dakota, but my dad and mom lived in Colorado at the time. My mom's siblings, who lived in South Dakota, dealt with most of the issues of their advancing age and health concerns.

I was frustrated, because even though it was clear that I wanted to broach topics of end-of-life care, neither my dad nor his doctor would discuss it. I do not know the root of my dad's physician's unwillingness to converse about the end of my dad's life. Did his physician's resistance to talk with candor during appointments stem from lack of education, discomfort, or inadequate insurance reimbursement? During office visits and the analysis of numbers on the latest blood draw, I wanted to shout that we were not discussing what really mattered. How could my sister, my dad's girlfriend, and I adequately care for him when he lived alone? At what point would it be impossible for him to live safely and independently? And at that point, what options were available?

I appreciated the way the authors of the article provided an analogy to explain hospice. "Patients need to be assured that a referral does not indicate that the physician has given up on them; rather, it will help them better understand their options. The physician might compare it to meeting with a financial planner to discuss hopes and goals for retirement."*

In my dad's last three months, he was surrounded by medical professionals. He did initially make progress with daily therapy, which improved his strength and mobility. As long as he was progressing towards goals, there was no prompt to discuss palliative care or the end of his life. However, his progression stopped abruptly when in October he was re-admitted to the hospital with severe pain, which was ultimately diagnosed as gallstones.

Communication also seemed lacking with doctors in the hospital. Side effects and risks of treatments were grossly under-acknowledged to both my dad and me. I felt pushed forward into his gall bladder surgery and other procedures without enough discussion of what could go wrong. Of course, someone always listed risks, but they were brushed over.

After gallbladder surgery, my dad struggled. He developed infections and pneumonia. After nearly two weeks in the hospital, he returned to the rehab center in a very sick state. If there was ever an ideal moment to initiate honest dialogue from medical professionals about the reality of his situation, that would have been the time.

I suspect his last week might have looked very different with hospice support. In the book *Changing The Way We Die*, authors Fran Smith and Sheila Himmel state, "Nobody wants to die badly. Hospice care offers the best hope for dying well and living fully until we do."

* http://www.mnmed.org/MMA/media/Minnesota-Medicine Magazine/Commentary_Baines_1502.pdf

Did my dad fool the medical professionals or were we involved with a system that avoided end-of-life discussions? Those conversations might have given my dad the opportunity to focus on last wishes, have meaningful conversations, and clarify his needs. There was a lost opportunity to facilitate healing and forgiveness between himself and his family. He only lived a few more weeks, and none of the staff gave me a clue during those final days that he was on death's doorstep.

CHAPTER TWENTY-ONE

Resisting Death

*"I don't want to achieve immortality through my work.
I want to achieve it through not dying."*
Woody Allen

I felt that my dad resisted death, fought to live on even when his quality of life was poor. During his last few years, he had a lot of pain and felt tired and depressed much of the time. He gradually stopped reading, quit listening to his favorite talk radio and TV programs, and complained that food had no taste and that he had no appetite. So many of the things that he loved were disappearing from his daily routine. He also started to lose bladder and bowel control, which resulted in accidents of ever-increasing frequency.

I grew more and more concerned that he was losing his dignity. He was always proud of his mental sharpness. When asked by staff at the rehab facility what the date was, he often did not know, and this would agitate him because he felt the questions were not showing his true intelligence. He sometimes told me that at night if he had trouble sleeping, he would practice Morse code in his mind.

Despite being diagnosed with dementia, my dad knew his family and friends' names and remembered the staff at the rehab center. His dementia was most likely vascular in origin, causing short-term memory issues and occasional bouts of confusion, but generally, he held onto his intellect. However, I saw his mind declining and I knew he sensed it too. I suspected that for him, losing his mental acuity was shameful and worse than incontinence. Diapers could be hidden under clothes, but the widening gaps in his ability to use his mind were difficult to hide and caused him distress.

I grew concerned that the longer he held onto life, the more his mind would slip. I feared that the loss of his mind would cause him humiliation. Part of me wished for his death to occur, before his mind left him completely, to preserve his dignity as much as was possible under the circumstances. In reality, his last conversation was with a night nurse he had met months before on another wing of the facility. She later told me that they had a pleasant conversation and that he was fully engaged in talking with her. Thankfully, he was lucid in the end, because I believe he valued his mind above all other physical functioning.

I often wondered why my dad continued to hold on to life so tightly when he had lost so much quality. From my perspective, surrendering might have brought him a peaceful conclusion to a long life. Since he appeared to resist dying, I acknowledged that there were multiple factors at work within him combined with his unique personality and history. For my own curiosity, I speculated about why he was reluctant to let go of life and found several possible answers. Most likely, he held on due to a combination of all of them.

Pure stubbornness

I wondered if his strong personality, which had the tendency towards pride, was sabotaging his spirit. Perhaps his inner soul was softer and more willing to let go but his dominant, stubborn ego wanted to fight on.

Unfinished business

In living a long life, it was possible my dad had some unresolved feelings, such as regrets or guilt. He may have been working through memories and feelings in his mind. His last relationship with his girlfriend was complex. They loved and cared deeply for one another, and they may also have had dynamics that fostered holding on to each other, making it difficult for either to grant permission to let go. I just acknowledged that they needed to work it out together on their own timetable.

Concern about leaving behind those he loved

His girlfriend was eighty when my dad died, and she had spent most every day with him or talked to him by phone for over a decade. Her life had begun to be defined by his companionship and care. I am fairly certain that my dad was concerned with how she would carry on after he left.

His kids and grandkids were more independent and busy with life, but he wanted reassurance that we would remember things he thought were important. He would quiz me about whether I had proper insurance coverage or if my daughters and I understood conservative politics. He would pester me not to forget where something was located, such as hidden tools in his truck that my daughter now drove. He wanted me to understand various facts, such as the best cut of beef or history of the lone survivor of the Battle of Little Bighorn (1876)—a horse named Comanche. And, of course, he wanted confirmation that his World War II memorabilia would be saved and cared for.

Fear of death and beyond

My dad never spoke about fear of death, but I wondered if he was frightened of it because he considered himself agnostic. He would not proclaim there was a God, but he wouldn't rule out the possibility of a Creator. I gathered from conversations we'd had together over the years that he felt death led to nothingness. You simply stopped living upon death and there was only blackness. He often said that life was not a dress rehearsal, implying that it was the final show and then it was over. No afterlife or soul immortality, heaven or reincarnation—the show was over!

Kathy Kalina, certified hospice and palliative nurse, wrote the book *Midwife for Souls: Spiritual Care for the Dying*. She mentions that those who have distanced themselves from God often struggle between the will and the spirit as death approaches. She states, "This is a time of choice, the ultimate choice—for God or against God. Patients who have lived as friends of God make this choice by second nature. Those who have lived alienated from him have a much harder time."

Faith in modern medicine to save him

My dad had faith in medicine. He hoped there would be a pill or procedure to fix or help his ailments. He once asked his doctor the pertinent question of whether his complaints were just the way it was in old age. His doctor was vague in his answer, preferring to give him hope by trying some sort of pharmaceutical adjustment. Perhaps because my dad never watched his parents grow old and had no siblings, he had no previous experience to draw upon for how life would look as one approached ninety. He had had two aunts who lived to over one hundred years of age, but he didn't see them often and had no direct experience with their day-to-day life.

A need to be cared for after having to be so strong his whole life

My dad grew up during the Great Depression, was an only child, and served in the Navy in World War II. He was ambitious and determined to be a successful businessman. He was driven to work hard and make large sums of money. He seemed to have something to prove. He was never satisfied with being typical. He wanted to be way above average and prosper. He desired to take good care of his family financially and leave an inheritance. I suspect that a life of such constant striving takes a toll. Perhaps he had reached a point where he was tired and wanted to be cared for by his family and nurses. I observed him expressing gratitude frequently to the caregiving staff at the nursing home. He may have had a need to soak up the care of people focusing on him after such a long life of responsibilities.

The ethic of "The Greatest Generation" and as a World War II veteran to fight to the very end

My dad never directly mentioned the quote of Britain's gallant Prime Minister Sir Winston Churchill, "Never, never,

never give up," but I know he admired him. So, based on the era in which my dad grew up, his history and beliefs, I suspect that he did not see any other choice but to fight to the very end. I also sensed my dad did not approve that his father took his own life. My dad modeled courage to take on anything that came his way. He may have decided that he would die a valiant fight until his last breath. He was part of a generation that showed bravery beyond our current day comprehension. Like Louie Zamperini in the book and movie *Unbroken*, he would not let the enemy defeat him. I suspect my dad felt death was the enemy and fought as long as he was able against it.

CHAPTER TWENTY-TWO

Costs of End-of-Life Care

"When you have to make a choice and don't make it,
that is in itself a choice."
William James

Karen Wyatt is the author of the book *What Really Matters: 7 Lessons for Living from the Stories of the Dying.* She mentions the financial and emotional side of our current healthcare system. "Approximately 25% of the annual Medicare budget is spent on aggressive, life-sustaining care during the final month of life, much of which is futile and may actually prolong suffering rather than enhance life."

On the financial side, my dad died just before the allowed Medicare coverage for rehabilitation expired after his hip fracture. I had scouted to find where he would reside after moving off the rehab wing and made the choice of a room for him on the skilled nursing side of the same facility. I was aware of the impending daily room cost and additional therapies. I also knew the high costs of his multiple surgeries, hospitalizations, ambulance rides, and doctor visits because our family received his bills showing what was covered and what was not. The sums were staggering. Medicare and his supplemental insurance covered most of the costs initially, but there were time limits to their coverage, and I knew that expenses would soon be coming out of his savings.

Holly G. Prigerson is the director of the Center for Psycho-oncology and Palliative Care Research at the Dana-Farber Cancer Institute at Harvard Medical School. She was quoted in a *Los Angeles Times* article entitled, "Choices at the End of Life." "We found that most of the costs of end-of-life care pay for burdensome, non-curative care that offers no substantial survival advantage." She continued, "We found that as the costs of care increase dramatically as death approaches, so too does the patient's emotional and physical suffering."[*]

The family and I also experienced mounting emotional strain after my dad's fall. Even though he was in a care facility, my visits had increased from one afternoon per week to three days each week. He never seemed to fully stabilize and needed more visits and care management than when he lived alone at home. I constantly ruminated about the long list of problems he seemed to have each day. I had to prioritize which issues seemed most pressing and figure out how to address them. I felt a growing sense of a losing battle. If one item was fixed, there were several new ones that sprang up to replace it. Often the issues were side effects of medications. The staff would experiment with different dosages and the times he received them. Sometimes they would discontinue the drug for a few days. Pain control, bowel consistency, and

---

[*] http://articles.latimes.com/2010/jan/22/health/la-he-end-of-life-costs25-2010jan25

skin irritations were a few of the many complaints my dad had after surgery.

Louis M. Profeta, M.D., is an emergency physician and author. In his article "I Know You Love Me, Now Let Me Die," he expresses concern about the mentality of our current path regarding end-of-life care in modern medicine. In the article he says, "A day does not go by where my partners don't look at each other and say, 'How do we stop this madness? How do we get people to let their loved ones die?'"**

October 2015 was my dad's last month of life, and ten days of it were in a hospital where he underwent two procedures for his gall bladder. He returned to rehab very weak and with mysterious infections and pneumonia. Less than a week after his discharge from the hospital to his rehab room, the staff wanted to send him back again. They said he could be monitored more closely in the hospital. I knew from recently seeing his telemetry machine that his heart had so many irregular beats and rhythms that the screen was in a constant state of alerts. I questioned if further analysis would lead anywhere but interventions. I feared ventilators, resuscitation, feeding tubes, and other aggressive life-sustaining care that would be administered if I allowed his return to the hospital. I didn't want his body to become a pincushion with tubes coming out of every orifice. I wanted to spare him broken ribs from CPR and shocks from defibrillators. I had reached the point of being willing to let him die.

Sadly, acceptance and surrender were not easy for my dad. He struggled physically and emotionally. He seemed increasingly miserable and dejected by the onslaught of health problems that were assaulting his weak body. He

---

** https://www.linkedin.com/pulse/i-know-you-love-me-now-let-die-louis-m-profeta-m

preferred to remain in bed as much as the staff would allow. At the same time, he seemed to want to carry on and fight.

My dad's last week was dark with unnecessary confusion and turmoil for him and for those he left behind. In hindsight, counseling at that point, or even earlier in my dad's struggle, might have brought a wider understanding of the big picture for him and our family. Acknowledging the emotional and financial costs of end-of-life care may have provided increased clarity for impending choices. Goals and decisions in light of the big picture may have helped the emotional welfare of all involved.

I believe it's imperative to bring the light of support and knowledge to patients and families when death is approaching. If a patient enters a hospital or other care facility with an incurable condition or high statistical probability of death, I promote clear and compassionate discussion. Angelo E. Volandes, M.D., has created a video outlining three end-of-life choices: life-prolonging care, limited medical care, or comfort care.*** I found this fabulous resource with research *after* my dad's death. If the push towards life-sustaining technology were balanced with options for comfort care in both medical school training and the healthcare culture, more people would have the chance to transition to death with dignity and grace. This balance might give more chances to say goodbye and find healing and closure.

*** http://theconversationbook.org

CHAPTER TWENTY-THREE

The Dying Process

"I'm still haunted by memories of tying patients down to keep them from pulling out tubes, repeatedly sticking IVs into worn-out arms, and assisting with heroic resuscitative measures that we called the 'million dollar send-off.'"
Kathy Kalina

Thankfully, my dad was spared the "million dollar send-off." Because I said no to hospitalizing him for increased monitoring in his final days, he did not undergo extreme measures to prolong his life. By reading Katy Butler and Barbara Karnes's books, I was growing in awareness and acceptance that his body was shutting down. I had decided to allow the process to continue without interference.

Prior to my dad's broken hip, he displayed withdrawal, diminished interest in food and increased sleep. He also complained of leg weakness. These symptoms often occur in the months prior to death. My dad had begun sleeping longer hours and had difficulty rising in the morning. On June 26, 2015, approximately a month before he fell, I wrote an email to my sister stating that his girlfriend called me because Dad had not answered his phone that morning. I let my sister know that he hadn't answered for me either. His girlfriend later called and said that he had just gotten up at 2:00 p.m.

July 28, 2015, after a visit to my dad, I wrote in an email to one of my dad's friends: "My dad had a very bad day. Doesn't want oxygen anymore or any life-prolonging measures. Wouldn't eat anything I brought. Has quit TV and radio during the day. Cried a lot. Talked about taking care of the kitties after he is gone." July 30, 2015, two days after that email, my dad fell and fractured his hip.

I read that in the weeks before death, often there will be disorientation and confusion, agitation and the physical changes of decreased blood pressure, fluctuating pulse and respiration, and complaints of being tired, to name a few. In the two weeks before my dad died, there was an episode where he saw a news story on the TV in his room and thought that his visitors sitting with him needed to call for help to assist the people in the news story. He became agitated when they did not act upon his plea. I also witnessed his eyes being glassy and half open as he sat in his wheelchair during his last week, and he told me he just wanted to go to bed on the last day I saw him. His feet were developing a purple hue from a lack of circulation despite being on constant oxygen.

I received calls from his nurse in the two days prior to his death about his fluctuating blood pressure and heart rate. That is when the nurse suggested he go to the ER, but I felt watching the roller coaster of his rhythms on a telemetry machine would be more stressful than focusing on his comfort. And, thankfully, he responded to the comfort measures that the nurse administered.

He had restlessness but also a surge of energy in the evenings of his last three days of life. Those flashes of energy were confusing to me because I thought perhaps he was improving. I also witnessed a detachment, as he was not inclined to talk to me much. On our last day together, he snapped at me, telling me he never wanted to do his breathing exercises again. Reflecting in the months after his death, I was able to not take that outburst personally. He might have been indicating that he was done and simultaneously distancing himself before leaving me behind.

He also mentioned to me that he was having weird dreams at night. He said he had been to a different place than where he was in the rehab facility. I wish I had asked more about that other place. I was exhausted and not of clear mind at that point, so I did not dig deeper for a description. But in retrospect, he may have had one foot in the next world and one foot in the earthly one.

Each person undergoes a unique process of dying and death, but those who work with terminal patients have seen patterns. Two books that were helpful to me to explain commonalities of progression were: *Gone From My Sight: The Dying Experience* by Barbara Karnes, RN, and *Midwife For Souls: Spiritual Care For The Dying* by Kathy Kalina.

No one was with my dad at the time of his death, so I do not know if he experienced specific symptoms of the dying process. Because it plagued me that I was not there when my dad died, I found comfort in Kathy Kalina's words, "If someone is not present at the time of death, it doesn't mean they've failed or that they're loved less than the ones who were there. The patient may have believed that seeing the death would be too hard for that person. Or perhaps the bond was so strong between them that the person's presence would have made leaving harder. Whatever the reason, remember: no one ever dies alone! Unseen friends from the other side, angels, and God himself assist the soul at the time of passage."

CHAPTER TWENTY-FOUR

What Age Is Ideal to Die?

"A dying man needs to die, as a sleepy man needs to sleep, and there comes a time when it is wrong, as well as useless, to resist."
Stewart Alsop

After my dad's death, I discovered the article in *The Atlantic* magazine entitled, "Why I hope to die at 75" by Ezekiel J. Emanuel.* At first I was shocked by his philosophy. Dr. Emanuel is an oncologist and American bioethicist and opposes legalized euthanasia.

In his article, Ezekiel J. Emanuel states, "Here is a simple truth that many of us seem to resist: living too long is also a loss. It renders many of us, if not disabled, then faltering and declining, a state that may not be worse than death but is nonetheless deprived. It robs us of our creativity and ability to contribute to work, society, the world. It transforms how

---

* http://www.theatlantic.com/magazine/archive/2014/10/why-i-hope-to-die-at-75/379329/

people experience us, relate to us, and, most important, remember us. We are no longer remembered as vibrant and engaged but as feeble, ineffectual, even pathetic."

After witnessing and experiencing my dad's decline as he approached ninety years of age, I re-evaluated my previous personal goal of living to one hundred or beyond. After he died, I spoke to those friends to whom I had previously mentioned my longevity goal and let them know that I was revising it. I told them I only want to live as long as my life is a quality life. I no longer care what number that represents.

In the United States, life expectancy at the time of this writing is approximately seventy-nine years, and depending on whether you are a male or female, it can be slightly more or less. Emanuel is not suggesting suicide or any other drastic measure to conclude his life at seventy-five. He is stating that he will view his healthcare differently at that point. Instead of doing all sorts of tests and treatments to prolong his life, he will stop most of them. No more colonoscopies or other cancer screens. Certainly no pacemaker or implantable defibrillator, bypass surgeries, or other heart surgeries. No more flu shots. Emanuel says, "Obviously, a do-not-resuscitate order and a complete advance directive indicating no ventilators, dialysis, surgery, antibiotics, or any other medication—nothing except palliative care even if I am conscious but not mentally competent—have been written and recorded. In short, no life-sustaining interventions. I will die when whatever comes first takes me."

Emanuel's view might offend some readers. His thoughts may not be in alignment with one's faith. His stand may be counter to the philosophy of becoming ageless. After all, most people take vitamins and other pills and potions that claim to be the ideal concoction to keep us going strong until a ripe old age. Some people become vegan or go gluten free or whatever the latest diet craze advocates. I am guilty of much of that thinking myself. But haven't we all heard about the vegetarian who drops dead of a heart attack or the smoker who never develops lung cancer?

Things are rarely black and white. If my dad had died from his first heart attack at age sixty-seven, we would not have mended our relationship and had some of the best times of our lives together. My daughters would never have met him and felt his influence shaping them. But after the first heart attack, which required no heroic measures other than hospitalization, there were other opportunities to die that my dad fought. One event was in August 2000, when he had another heart attack at age seventy-nine. He was about to check out of the hotel where he had been staying in San Diego. He had just enjoyed a fabulous steak dinner with his cousin and other relatives after watching the horse races in Del Mar. As he approached the hotel desk in the lobby to check out, he experienced chest pain and the hotel personnel called for an ambulance. They determined at the hospital that he needed immediate triple bypass surgery.

My brothers flew to San Diego to be with him post-op. They reported to me that my dad was extremely angry when he woke up from surgery. They recounted to me that they perceived he was mad to still be alive and suffering so much pain. He had almost accidentally orchestrated a perfect way to go. Having just enjoyed a fabulous vacation and a terrific steak dinner, he was on the spike of a high note to exit life. But modern medicine saved him. Perhaps his doctors wondered why he wasn't happy with their successful intervention.

He gradually recovered from the second major heart event, albeit with heart damage and the wind knocked out of his sails. Such a perfect exit never presented itself again. In his last year of life, he had so many medications that my dad could no longer handle filling his pillbox organizer accurately. My sister created a sheet that listed each pill, what it looked like, and whether it was a morning or evening pill. My sister and I traded off filling his box for him, and it took our utmost concentration to do so correctly. Often the pills had to be altered due to side effects or ineffectiveness. There were pills for his heart, his thyroid, his arthritis pain, his depression, his prostate issues, and his blood pressure. Additionally, there were diuretics, vitamins, and nutritional supplements. He swallowed enough pills each day to make me gag just thinking about it.

I could say that his first heart attack offered him a chance to make improvements to his closest family relationships, which he did. I am forever grateful that we had such an opportunity. I might say that he missed a great finale when he lived through the second heart event in San Diego, yet, because he lived beyond his bypass surgery, our family had the chance to spend memorable moments with him. My daughters and I took some fabulous trips with him for multiple years in a row to Hawaii between 2001 and 2005, often visiting his naval ship together. And he and I returned to Del Mar and watched the horse races each August, from 2006 through 2009. The final year he went to Del Mar in 2009, my girls joined us for the races too. Those were special times for all of us.

Dad rebounded and experienced fairly good health in his seventies and early eighties. But all travel and most quality ended in 2010, when at age eighty-four, he suffered a stroke.

He was lucky because he could still walk and do basic self-care after his stroke and was able to return to his beloved home. But reading became difficult and driving was not encouraged. He required a walker or cane, and all bodily systems seemed tired and worn out. With a predisposition not to be a regular exerciser anyway, he had difficulty exercising due to pain. He became sedentary and progressively weaker.

Due to his confinement to a home out in the country without being able to travel, he became lonely. He suffered depression and despair. In my opinion, he had reached a tipping point. Most of the things he loved to do were no longer possible. Yet, he seemed to hold on to life more tightly.

His relationships became strained. He relied on his girlfriend, my sister, and me to do more and more things for him and to take on the role of caregivers. The last stroke was like a torpedo hitting his ship. The ship was going down and would take some passengers with it. He would not leave his home, and he didn't want home healthcare coming in either.

My dad had an elongated dying process. Emanuel argues that society and families might be better off if nature took its course swiftly and promptly. Along the way, it certainly would have behooved me to ask more about the risks of complications and potential negative results from interventions and surgeries. I wish I had questioned the chances of infection, pneumonia, as well as drug and anesthetic reactions to bring more light to potential choices or side effects and to weigh gain verses risk. In hindsight, I might not have encouraged his last surgery, the removal of his gall bladder, after all.

Today, I have more knowledge and my research after my dad's death has opened my eyes to new choices for my future healthcare. I may elect to forego major medical tests and interventions after a certain age. My focus will be for quality years rather than quantity. At a certain point, I may let nature take its course in my body and accept my mortality as gracefully as I am able to do so. Surrendering to the best of my abilities when the price of life has outweighed its benefit may be a compassionate choice for me and those around me.

CHAPTER TWENTY-FIVE

The Stuff We Collect

"Maturity is a process of subtraction, not addition."
M. Chadbourne

Marie Kondo has written two books on tidying up—*The Life-Changing Magic of Tidying Up* and *Spark Joy*. In *Spark Joy*, she boldly states, "Life truly begins only after you have put your house in order." She advocates discarding first and keeping only what sparks joy for you or what is useful. She provides the order to tidy and then describes how to organize and store what is left. She says, "When you put your house in order, you put your affairs and your past in order too. As a result, you can see quite clearly what you need in life and what you don't, and what you should and shouldn't do."

When my youngest daughter graduated from high school in 2012, I downsized my home. I had to dramatically reduce my stuff to fit into my new house. I went from a three-car garage to no garage. I still sometimes miss my bicycle, but now I borrow a friend's bike or rent one if I want to ride. Instead of a massive bookshelf, multiple file cabinets, and a large desk in a home office, I now use the corner of my dining room table for my laptop, since my new home has no office. I also went from a walk-in clothes closet to a small one that required me to get rid of 75% of my clothes.

I am a book lover, and before I moved and downsized my living space, I had a plethora of books. Like my clothes, I had to get rid of most of them to fit into my smaller house. Marie Kondo's suggests that, "We read books because we seek the experience of reading. Once read, a book has already been 'experienced'."

Because I was immersed in my own process of reducing the amount of stuff in my life, I started to look at my dad's files and papers a year or so prior to his death. In his declining health, it had become obvious that he did not have the energy or desire to sort his files. So I took boxes of files home and tried to make sense of them.

At home with his files, I spread them out on my dining room table to sort. I found files of clippings on things that interested him, such as Ronald Reagan or saddles. Most of these files were of no appeal to anyone but him, and sadly, he had gradually stopped reading in the last year of his life. So many files went into the trash bin, and it was a long and tedious exercise that took me months. When I thought I had made headway, I would find a stash of articles stuffed into the drawer of his nightstand or some other unlikely article-storing location.

The same held true for his photography. My dad loved photographs. He took a lot of pictures with his camera, and other people took many shots of him. When he had the pictures printed, he usually ordered multiple copies. When I sorted my dad's paper files, I also gathered his photos. Since he had an obsession with duplicate pictures, he decided to scatter them all through the house in obscure locations. He didn't take much time to organize these pictures into albums for easy viewing; they were placed loose in boxes. He seemed to think that if he had ten of the same photo, he should make sure they were in ten different locations throughout the house, perhaps in case something happened to one of the locations. Finding these stashes of photos when I had already spent a ridiculous amount of time organizing and scanning the ones I had previously located started to drive me crazy.

In the year prior to his death on my Tuesday afternoon visits, I often asked my dad questions about photos I was sifting through. Since my dad was an only child, he was the only one who could identify others in old pictures and tell the stories behind the scenes. So I asked him to write names, years, or locations on the backs of the photos. His long-term memory was still quite remarkable even when his short-term memory became fuzzy. After months of photo sorting and labeling, I digitally scanned them and then put the pictures in albums or in marked envelopes. I continued on out of respect for my dad and my personal love of family history.

In all honesty, I wished my dad had done this sorting task himself. Part of the time I felt resentment at the chaos I was organizing. In his last years, my dad spent most of his waking hours at his dining room table staring out the window, listening to talk radio, or watching political programs on the television set located in that room. When I arrived at his home for lunch each Tuesday, his dining table always had stacks of newspapers, magazines, mail, folders, and books. It appeared to me to be a mess that grew by the week and it irritated me to look at it while we ate lunch amongst it. Many times after we finished eating, I attempted to engage him in the process of sorting. I would grab one of the many piles of papers on the table and ask him what we should do with it. He would say he was too tired to look at it. When he retired to his bedroom for an afternoon nap and I was left alone at the table of papers, I began to wade through them.

My dad did not declutter or downsize. He did not like to tidy up his living space. He had trouble discarding junk mail, old newspapers, and magazines, not to mention clothes he would never wear again, or other broken, worn out, and obsolete items. His attitude that he couldn't be bothered with discarding and the assumption that it would ultimately be my job to empty his house grated on me. Often I would return to my own home and launch into a tidying frenzy, because I felt stifled at not being able to make progress with my dad's stuff.

Because my dad had not thinned out meaningless clutter from his home in his later years of life, I felt I could not savor the experience of finding something cool that I might treasure when I cleared out his home in the months after his death. It was an arduous process for me to do for him. There was a massive amount of stuff and a fairly short window of time to empty his home. The sheer excessive volume of clutter combined with my grief created a heavy experience for me as I went from room to room to clear out what he'd left behind.

Fortunately, that cycle has stopped. The difficult experience of cleaning out my dad's house created an impetus to make a change in my personal situation. My girls will hopefully find my house in excellent order. I still continually thin out and organize what remains to lessen the future burden for them when it is their time to empty my home upon my death. By watching me regularly sort my things, I trust that I am modeling to them how to release items that no longer serve a purpose in their lives and how to avoid accumulating stuff. I regularly suggest they sort their clothes and belongings to give away what no longer fits, feels good, or uplifts them.

The process of decreasing the quantity of my household items was liberating, and I have no desire to go back to a larger space. I enjoy my home more when I have tidied my possessions, keeping only what is useful and gives me pleasure.

CHAPTER TWENTY-SIX

Loss and Grief

"Grief offers us all an opportunity to pause and look at the deeper questions of life, to find personal meaning and purpose."
Sameet M. Kumar, PH.D.

Sameet Kumar, Ph.D., is a clinical psychologist for the Memorial Cancer Institute in Broward County, Florida. He specializes in working with cancer patients and their caregivers. In his book, *Grieving Mindfully*, Kumar says, "Although loss often makes you feel as if a door has closed on a relationship, in time you will see that actually a new door has opened—one that leads to the rest of your life." Grief is part of my human experience. There will always be loss during my lifetime. Loss has come in a variety of forms to me—such as death, divorce, losing a job, and selling a beloved home. Each event brought me new opportunities and experiences that would not have been possible otherwise. Kumar summarizes the process well. "Grieving mindfully can be understood as making the decision to allow yourself to mourn, and to fully experience the lessons of grief with the goal of living life better."

The word "mindful" essentially means to be focused on the present moment. Before my dad died, I worried—reviewing what had just transpired or planning next steps obsessively. This fretting kept me awake at night and never allowed my mind to rest. None of my ruminating helped me. Instead, it took me to the brink of exhaustion and collapse. While his health declined, taking trips on occasion helped me to rest my mind and focus on new landscapes and experiences. Thankfully, I had a beach vacation shortly after his death, which provided me an opportunity to practice mindfulness at a critical point of being overwhelmed and fatigued. The sounds, sights, and smells of the sea felt like soothing balm to my overworked mind and grieving heart.

Over the years, I was aware of the stages of grief from books written by Elisabeth Kübler-Ross. Denial, anger, bargaining, depression, and acceptance are the stages Kübler-Ross outlines and describes. In the book she co-authored with David Kessler, *On Grief and Grieving*, she explains why it is important to grieve. "Why grieve? For two reasons. First, those who grieve well, live well. Second, and most important, grief is the healing process of the heart, soul, and mind; it is the path that returns us to wholeness. It shouldn't be a matter of if you will grieve; the question is when will you grieve. And until we do, we suffer from the effects of that unfinished business."

Grief tends to weave in and out of my days in unpredictable ways. Certain events, such as holidays, birthdays, or anniversaries, can summon moments of sadness. Other times I am caught off guard by hearing certain songs on the radio, finding a picture or memento, or bumping into a mutual friend. My dad loved to jitterbug. I will never forget seeing him dance with his girlfriend to "In the Mood" by Glenn Miller in front of the USS Missouri when we attended the 60th anniversary celebration of the end of World War II. When the song was played at a dance in my local community the summer after his death, I was flooded with the memories of seeing him dance. I kept the visualization in my mind as I did the jitterbug myself—accompanied by wet eyes.

With time, those triggers lose their punch and the emotions pass more swiftly. Kessler and Kübler-Ross also say, "The reality is that you will grieve forever. You will not 'get over' the loss of a loved one; you will learn to live with it. You will heal, and you will rebuild yourself around the loss you have suffered. You will be whole again, but you will never be the same. Nor should you be the same, nor would you want to."

When I resisted grief or wallowed in it, I felt worse during those big disruptions in my life. I believe that what I focus on tends to grow and acts like a magnet. After my divorce and the death of my dad, if I met with my friends and only talked about my despair, I felt worse afterwards. Furthermore, I usually created an atmosphere that reminded them of their hurts, and together we magnified the woes of our lives. Now, with my growing awareness of how to facilitate healing, I acknowledge my grief in conversations but then shift to measures I am taking to feel better. I talk about how I moved from complete exhaustion and sadness to feeling flat and then to feeling a spark of new life. I also share what I am learning or a memory that has surfaced. I have discovered many ways to still acknowledge loss, but I practice subtle changes in how I frame my words to keep making progress. If I leave the meeting upbeat, I know my practice is working.

David Singer, in his book *The Untethered Soul,* talks about pain as a temporary disturbance. Others call it impermanent. Singer states, "If you want to be free, simply view inner pain as a temporary shift in your energy flow. There is no reason to fear this experience. Pain is a thing in the universe that is passing through your system." In the past, I have regrettably kept pain locked inside for far too long. My own divorce was where I felt the most challenged in letting go. The pain resulting from the loss of my marriage kept me in victim mode and sometimes became my identity. It was all I thought about, talked about, and wrote about for a long time! I can now look back and realize that I wasted years of my life holding onto that heartbreak. It was incredibly liberating to heal and move on. Singer suggests letting disturbances pass through us like the wind. Easier said than done, especially with big events such as divorce and death, but when I think about the wind analogy, it does encourage stagnant sorrow to move out.

I have given myself permission to deeply and completely mourn the loss of my dad. If I need to cry, I let the tears flow. Sometimes I save them for private moments because I feel more able to let go without worrying about how my emotions are affecting someone else. Gradually my grief has lightened.

As time passes, I give sadness less and less of my attention and instead I switch my focus to what is alive, what is beautiful, and what is before me now. I look more closely at the clouds in the sky and the colors of nature around me. I listen more attentively to music and savor the tastes of my favorite foods. That shift in my view and my energy has made my life much more pleasant today. When I contemplate life as well as death, I am discovering what really matters to me now. My relationship with my family and friends is a high priority.

Simplifying my life so I feel less stretched with obligations gives me more of a chance to linger where I please and do what I most enjoy. And I am seizing the opportunity to go on dream trips that have been on my bucket list, such as seeing live professional tennis at the US Open in New York City.

I can always trace good things that have come to me after a loss that have added positively to my life today. I have met new friends and connected more deeply with those already in my life. As I inch forward to embrace my life again by being mindful, writing books, and planning adventures, I sense my dad would approve. I know he would want me to be happy.

CHAPTER TWENTY-SEVEN

Forgiveness

"Holding on to anger, resentment and hurt only gives you tense muscles, a headache and a sore jaw from clenching your teeth. Forgiveness gives you back the laughter and the lightness in your life."
Joan Lunden

I believe one of the most important reasons I am here today is to practice forgiveness and to learn the power of it as a gift to others and myself. By focusing on forgiveness in my life today, I am promoting my healing and lessening my regrets. Some of my dad's behavior created opportunities for me to practice forgiveness, as did a number of other events in my life. The human experience seems ripe for me to step up to this challenge.

Ira Byock, M.D., a pioneer in the American hospice movement, describes forgiveness well. "Many people confuse forgiveness with exoneration. Forgiveness does not excuse someone from doing something wrong. It does not alleviate their guilt or lessen their transgression. Instead, forgiveness accepts the past as it was, embraces the present, and faces the future. Forgiveness is a strategy for you to become free of emotional baggage. Hate, fury, recrimination, and blame weigh us down. The ball and chain of old wounds tethers us to the past and limits our ability to move forward with vitality."

Dr. Byock wrote the book *The Four Things That Matter Most*. Those four things are statements:

Please forgive me.
I forgive you.
Thank you.
I love you.

I said "I love you" verbally to my dad when he was about to undergo his hip surgery, in the pre-op waiting room just before they wheeled him off to the surgical suite. He returned with, "I love you too, Babe." We did not have the type of relationship where "I love you" was said regularly, but I was glad we did say it then. When I cleaned his things from his house, I also found notes and cards where we wrote "I love you" to each other on occasions such as birthdays and Father's Day.

Prior to my dad's hip surgery, he regularly thanked me for my visits. His demeanor and attitude changed when he was in the rehab facility, and he was often critical and unkind. That change stung, and I became apprehensive when I walked into his room. One of his doctors used the term "emotionally stabbing" to describe my dad's behavior towards me. His physician told me that one person close to the parent often gets the brunt of all the person's frustration, anger, and blame, which results in verbalizing inappropriate words that the recipient might find hurtful.

In rehab over the following several weeks after his hip fracture, he was particularly harsh to me, and I felt deflated and unappreciated. I will always cherish a heartfelt apology I received after several rough visits. It came as he sat in his wheelchair and I was sitting on a bench outside the front door of the rehab center. He told me he appreciated all I did to help him. He said that he knew he was in a good place with good therapists and staff. He admitted it might be where he needed to be. I was able to swallow built-up resentment and graciously accept his apology and his thanks. His courage and ability to express himself was a gift to me, and the power of it still lingers to this day. I know in my heart that he was grateful for my constant presence, but due to pain, fear, episodes of dementia, and a reserved upbringing, he had trouble expressing himself. I will be forever grateful for that day. It meant everything to me.

Dr. Byock's four statements seem simple, but they were not consistently practiced with my dad and me throughout our lives. Reflecting on the occasions when we were able to say those powerful words, I treasure the times when we were able to break through our discomfort or turmoil of challenging circumstances and express those healing phrases.

Self-forgiveness has also been a work in progress for me. As I reflected after my dad's death, I had to dispel the thoughts of "I didn't say or do enough" and instead remind myself of all I did do. In my mind, I wrestled with the decision to allow his final gall bladder surgery. If I had said no to the second procedure, he might have been able to rebound for a while longer. Instead, he was plagued with infection, developed pneumonia, and never regained the strength and progress he had made in his rehabilitation the week prior. And I have pondered my decision to go home when I thought the end was near. Curbing those futile thoughts and shifting to self-forgiveness is easier said than done. It requires vigilance not to allow my mind to dwell on those decisions.

Writing this book has been an exercise in self-forgiveness. It has forced me to remember and relive events that I would rather have forgotten. But it has also widened my view of my dad's life. Dad and I did not have a good last day together. But dwelling on that interaction does not do justice to the entirety of our relationship. Instead of fixating on the last few years, months, and days, I expanded my vision and memories to his whole life. It wasn't just me making decisions. Every decision he made throughout his life influenced his health and the circumstances he found himself in as he aged. I entered the picture in the eleventh hour as a guide to the exit of his life. I navigated as best I could the role of end-of-life shepherd—a journey that I had never taken before. I have to forgive myself for what I did not know. And I have to forgive him for the times that he felt unequipped to deal with the unknown.

After my dad's death, I researched and read books by others who were caregivers or doctors. I was able to identify with their plights and felt compassion for their tales. In turn, it helped me feel compassion for myself. I appreciated their honesty as they shared the imperfect nature of healthcare. A story sometimes showed that they had taken a left- instead of a right-hand turn in the waning days of someone's life, and it did not turn out well. I also read accounts where bad choices ended up being blessings in disguise.

To me, life feels like a lonely road unless we are willing to risk the possibility of connecting heart to heart. So, as I think about forgiveness of my dad and myself, centered on his death, I have found that I am more aware of forgiveness in my everyday life. When I encounter someone who is crabby, I attempt to look through the behavior to the possible pain that might lie behind it. I realize that each person has struggles in their lives and on some days, it is hard to hide. I also acknowledge that I have snapped at people on a day where my ability to cope was not fortified.

Forgiveness is a big topic, and I cannot begin to touch on all the facets of it other than to acknowledge that it is probably the most challenging task I have in living. But I have made progress by investing in it. Dr. Byock talks about the emotional toll of non-forgiveness. "It is wrong to think that people need to feel forgiveness in order to give forgiveness. Forgiveness is actually about emotional economics. It's about a one-time cost that you pay to clear up years of compounded emotional pain. It's like taking a one-time loss in financial investments. Refusing to forgive means accepting the cost of the hurts inflicted on you compounded a thousand times. And it means carrying them forever as they accrue in negative emotional energy."

I am certain that I'm not the only one who would like to have a do-over on an interaction with a loved one. It was challenging to snap my fingers and suddenly *feel* better about our last day together. But when I become aware of the memory of words we spoke that still carry a feeling of heaviness, I practice *giving* forgiveness to my dad and myself. I sometimes have to repeat my thought of *giving* forgiveness multiple times before the scene in my mind has lighter energy surrounding it. The shift from thinking that I must *feel* forgiveness to the practice of repetitive *giving* of forgiveness has helped me in my healing journey.

CHAPTER TWENTY-EIGHT

Awareness and Change

*"Learn to get in touch with the silence within yourself
and know that everything in this life has a purpose."*
Elisabeth Kübler-Ross

When I was enmeshed in the final year of my dad's life, I was unnecessarily lost in the dark. I craved help. He was rapidly declining but still lived independently yet precariously in his home. I reached out to his primary care physician begging for honest dialogue about my dad's mortality. His physician preferred conversation about tests and medicine changes. My dad stubbornly fought for a life of diminishing quality. His progressive weakness and fatigue placed him in unsafe situations as he navigated through his home with stairs and obstacles. He ate less and less and was increasingly unable to perform basic activities of daily living by himself. He and our family needed help.

Atul Gawande, practicing surgeon and author of *Being Mortal*, reveals the struggles of his profession. He discusses in the introduction of his book the views he acquired in medical school. "The way we saw it, and the way our professors saw it, the purpose of medical schooling was to teach how to save lives, not how to tend to their demise." He went on to say, "I am in a profession that has succeeded because of its ability to fix. If your problem is fixable, we know just what to do. But if it's not? The fact that we have no adequate answers to this question is troubling and has caused callousness, inhumanity, and extraordinary suffering."

In my dad's last month of life, after a ten-day interruption for gall bladder surgery and the ensuing complications post-surgery, the staff tiptoed around the truth of his condition. No one would utter the idea that my dad might not recover. No one talked about the stages a body goes through when nearing death. The staff performed their care tasks as they had been taught.

As Dr. Gawande matured in his practice and experienced the death of his own father, as well as some patients along the way, he started to examine the shortcomings and failures of treating the aging and dying. He investigated hospice and nursing home reformers. He then revealed his findings. "Our reluctance to honestly examine the experience of aging and dying has increased the harm we inflict on people and denied them the basic comforts they most need. Lacking a coherent view of how people might live successfully all the way to their very end, we have allowed our fates to be controlled by the imperatives of medicine, technology, and strangers."

After my dad's death, I wondered how others had broached delicate topics and navigated the tumultuous end-of-life care decisions. I was relieved to find the book *The Conversation: A Revolutionary Plan for End-of-Life Care,* by Angelo E. Volandes, M.D. Not only does he advocate meaningful discussions, he has created videos to help his patients start the process of thoughtful dialogue to express what they want. He queries his patients about what is most important to them, what gets them out of bed in the morning, what makes them happy, and what they are looking forward to most. Some of his patients responded that they had never previously been asked what they wanted.

He then asked about their fears of getting sick or needing medical care and if any specific medical treatment would be too much for them. He questioned what symptoms would be difficult to accept or make life not worth living. He clarified the patient's thoughts about quantity verses quality of life. He drilled down to the core of their beliefs and wishes about end-of-life care. If the conversation felt premature to the patient, the questions and answers could be considered and written down and sent in a letter or email to a loved one for future reference.

I never heard a doctor ask my dad those types of questions. As his daughter, and the one who had been appointed the Medical Power of Attorney, it felt as if he would perceive that I expected or wanted him to die if I asked him those questions. Based on his past behavior, his occasional bouts of irrational thought, and the tenuous nature of our relationship, the risk of initiating such a conversation felt too daunting. A medical professional might have bridged the gap, providing an atmosphere of neutrality while preserving our delicate connection.

When a previous doctor dared to approach the subject of God with my dad, my dad's reaction was to fire him. I gingerly brought up the topic a few times in the hopes of sharing my thoughts related to the soul living on after death, but he seemed unable to discuss or acknowledge the possibility. However, a few weeks before my dad passed, I was sitting with him in the hospital before his gall bladder surgery. A chaplain came into the room and began pleasant conversation with my dad. I braced myself, not knowing how my dad would react. He was amicable in return. The chaplain then asked if we could all pray together. To my surprise, my dad said yes. The three of us held hands and bowed our heads as a prayer was recited. After the chaplain departed, my dad said to me, "I guess it can't hurt." This comment indicated to me an opening in his previously closed stance.

Despite this one-time chaplain visit, my experience of witnessing our current hyper-medicalized culture showed a lack in integration of the spiritual dimension. My dad was at an incurable and terminal point in his life. I would have liked the opportunity for counseling, guidance, and prayer during his transition. I will never know what it might have done for my dad. It is possible that he would have declined further spiritual counseling as the end drew near, but I would have accepted it if it had been more readily offered.

Ideally, I would like to see the medical profession and the insurance industry move towards a greater emphasis and support of palliative care and hospice. Palliative care is defined as specialized medical care for people with serious illness. It focuses on providing relief from the symptoms and stress of a serious illness. The goal is to improve quality of life for both the patient and the family.[*] A paradigm shift of viewing palliative care or hospice as a gift instead of seeing it as giving up has the potential to change the way we experience advanced age. Without guidance and support for patients and families approaching death, there may be unnecessary conflict, confusion, and trauma that linger long after the passing of a loved one. If palliative care or hospice is the norm, the standard protocol, and endorsed by insurance, death may foster closeness and healing that positively impacts our society and our views of death.

Currently, hospice is a Medicare benefit for those wishing to forego attempts at curative treatments and for patients whose doctors have estimated that they have fewer than six months to live. A few friends have told me stories of how hospice was a godsend to the last days of their parent's life. I find myself speechless after hearing the vast difference in our experiences. When I reflect on the stories of death supported by hospice care and contrast it with our story depicting an absence of support, I find myself dealing with envy and anger. I have channeled those emotions into this book with the hope that hearing our story might give someone else a chance to create a better ending to the life of a loved one.

Ideally, it would be standard practice for doctors to discuss end-of-life stages and offer options of care for the elderly and those with incurable, terminal conditions. It is possible that healthcare costs might be reduced if the risks of life-prolonging procedures were properly explained and understood by families. The option of comfort care might become more attractive than aggressive treatments.

Because medical science has advanced, providing antibiotics, surgical remedies, and a multitude of

---

* https://getpalliativecare.org/whatis/

pharmaceutical treatments, life expectancy has risen over the last one hundred years. As the public perceives that a longer life expectancy is a good thing, we may not realize that the dying process has perhaps become more difficult. Marilyn Webb, author of *The Good Death: The New American Search to Reshape the End of Life*, states, "Medical success may have even allowed death to become more hidden, lulling Americans into losing knowledge not just of the physical process of dying, but of the psychological and spiritual dimensions of death."

I am still a bit amazed that I only learned about physical changes that the body undergoes prior to death from an email a friend sent to me. I had told him about my concern regarding my dad's fragile health. He had lost his father a few years prior and asked if I knew anything about the dying process. I acknowledged that I was not familiar with it. So he shared with me an overview of *Gone From My Sight: The Dying Experience* by Barbara Karnes, RN. As I read the stages my dad was entering, I marveled that I had reached fifty years of age and was just now being exposed to a concept that is part of every human experience. I found it remarkable that despite my physical therapy training, I had never been taught about the body's dying process. My education had been focused on making the patient better, always working towards progressive goals of more function and mobility. The dying stages were never explained to my dad either.

I did succeed in saying no to a proposed trip to the ER that I suspect might have led to his being hooked up to life support machines. His life had dipped to an ever-increasing diminished quality, but it might have become a living hell if excessive measures to prolong his life were begun.

Webb concludes her book by stating, "Modern medicine may have made dying harder, but it has also given us the gift of time—the time to prepare, the time to heal family wounds, the time to bring psychological and spiritual closure. If we can take advantage of it, it has given us something unique in history: the time to tie up loose ends and orchestrate a death that is good."

CHAPTER TWENTY-NINE

Obituaries

*"I don't think most people know what's going to be
in their obituary, but I do."*
Robert Mankoff

My dad wrote his own obituary about a decade before he died. This decision indicated that intellectually he knew he would ultimately die, but somehow as it actually got closer, he appeared to me to push away from death. Nonetheless, I had his obituary in my hands and began to prepare to publish it upon his death. Because I am a writer, I enhanced it and made some basic alterations for readability. I created a draft on my computer and tweaked it here and there, adding pictures and a video to bring it to life for future readers. I appreciated that he gave me this foundation to work with and decided I should do that for my own daughters. So, I drafted my own obituary for them and placed it in a document folder that can be accessed at the time of my death.

Some people might say they have no interest in writing their own obituary, especially if they are in good health. One might say that it is morbid or depressing. I feel it provides a thought-provoking exercise of introspection. How do I summarize my life thus far? By doing so, I have opportunities to make adjustments today and tomorrow through my choices that will affect an updated obituary later. It is a chance to make changes NOW! And a side benefit is that my loved ones will have a basic foundation to expand upon later instead of creating stress as they try to figure out what to say when they may not know my history as well as I do.

I underestimated the power of this exercise as a way to reflect on how far I have come. When I sat down to write mine, I reviewed my life thus far. I remembered my roots and beginnings, dreams and directions. I evaluated my accomplishments in my mind and then put to paper the facts and events I wanted to highlight. Of course there were failures along the way, but I didn't mention many setbacks, because I believe my life is more about overcoming challenges than letting difficulties define me.

I then gave myself a chance to contemplate my future by thoughtfully visualizing the rest of the story. I asked myself what adjustments I could make now. I let my mind create images of what would give me satisfaction and minimize regret. I entertained how I could be of service or contribute to my circle of friends, family, and community. I pondered what people might say at a memorial service or celebration. I asked myself how I would ideally like to be described and remembered.

Of course, I only wrote my obituary up until now. But the exercise of writing it helped me gain clarity about how I want to live today and tomorrow. I relish celebrating everything that comes my way. I also find myself more aware of my choices. I feel a zeal for completing projects. I look for what I have not finished, and I complete it. I tidy up messes—house clutter as well as financial clutter. I look at the moments I spend with my family or friends as opportunities to say what needs to be said, clear up misunderstandings, and express appreciation or love. I also find myself letting go of some relationships or redefining them. As my life direction evolves, I sometimes shift my time and align my attention toward different people and pursuits.

I know what is contained in my obituary so far, and I have a vision for the rest of my story. I feel increased confidence to take steps to make my vision a reality, progressing to the best of my abilities for as long as I have left.

CHAPTER THIRTY

His Lasting Legacy

"Other things may change us, but we start
and end with the family."
Anthony Brandt

In 1992, as I approached thirty and my dad sixty-seven, the call I got that he'd had a heart attack was the beginning of a change in both our lives in a big way. We were given a second chance. We had the opportunity to re-evaluate our relationship and invest more into it.

Tom Brokaw's book *The Greatest Generation*, had not yet been written in 1992. At that time, I didn't comprehend the magnitude of my dad's survival through the Great Depression and World War II. Prior to his heart attack, I'd been busy, working, married, and in my late twenties. We were each fairly self-absorbed in our separate lives.

Over the years, there were more heart attacks and strokes. Each event took some wind out of his sails, but he had an uncanny way of surviving the assaults until nearly ninety years of age. I am thankful that my daughters and I were able to learn more about him and his past. We now have an appreciation of WWII history and, in particular, his ship, the USS Missouri. We also have a basic understanding of ranching and agriculture, despite our disinterest in actually living that lifestyle personally. We have heard his views on politics, even if we don't fully engage in the same stances he held.

I love the music from the Big Band Era and am glad I got to swing dance with him a few times. The girls and I love visiting his hometown of Wessington Springs, South Dakota.

I share in his appreciation for animals. My dad loved to feed the hummingbirds and count and watch the geese that came to his ranch. I admire the way he loved his cats and the dogs he had along the way. He was kind to them and they loved him back.

Since my dad was involved in insurance and was a stickler for car maintenance, I always carry sufficient insurance, check the oil, and rotate my tires. I used to be dragged to the Stock Show and other cowboy and western type events. I was more of a city girl and just didn't care much for the western life he was moving into upon his retirement. It turns out some of that western stuff stuck to me, in that I do enjoy country western dancing. I may not be a lover of horseback riding, but there is a little cowgirl in me after all!

I don't remember ever eating his mom Jane's chicken firsthand, but Dad did a good job making it himself for years. His ranch meals were greatly anticipated—chicken, corn, mashed potatoes, baked beans, and corn bread. Jane's salad dressing—vinegar, milk, and sugar—was served on lettuce. He wanted me to remember to have a little tomato juice before the meal and pass the pickles whether I liked them or not. At some point, he would lean back in his chair and proclaim, "It doesn't get much better than this!" or "Pity the poor folks eating at the country club."

I will always remember that Dad *always* had a glass of milk after every meal—and somebody better jump up and get it for him, pronto! He loved my homemade vanilla ice cream and would have three helpings when it was first served soft just after I made it. I was glad to be able to make him several batches in his last few months, which brought him great enjoyment. Sometimes all we need are the simple things.

Dad loves milk

The kids often got gifts—Crackerjacks or Sacajawea coins, and sometimes Pendleton blankets. Occasionally, he gave out two-dollar bills, which I liked to give as tips for coffee or drinks.

My dad clipped articles that he was sure we needed to read and put them in our mail slot at his house. Reading all the articles seemed overwhelming at times, but I knew that Dad wanted me to be informed and understand key issues that were important to him. He also cultivated in me a love of paper maps. Looking at all the possible routes and pit stops on road trips is fun.

I laugh at the fact that he used his dining table as his desk, because that is what has happened to me. And I sometimes set important papers on the kitchen floor just like he did!

My daughters had a little over twenty years of their lives to get to know him. Here are their words about what he meant to each of them.

Going to visit Grandpa at the ranch was always an experience, a sort of trip back in time to a different way of life and set of values. Just a forty-minute drive from our house in Denver took us to a whole different world, right to the center of what it means to be American, to live in the West, to be a cowboy. One of my most treasured memories as a kid going to Grandpa's ranch was sitting on top of a cattle gate with my sister, Liberty, as we took a break from our explorations, looking out at the blue sky and the grass on the hills waving in the wind. The ranch took my breath away every time I went out there. Our Fourth of July trips to Grandpa's ranch in South Dakota were even a whole other level of special. Being in Wessington Springs, I'd feel time slow down and life get simpler, needing nothing more than the diving board at the pool and soft serve ice cream at the Humm-Dinger to make me happy.

While Liberty and I were out exploring at the ranch or building up our fort, the lunch bell would eventually summon us back to Grandpa's house where we knew a great meal was awaiting us. Whenever I travel out of the country and am asked to describe the typical American meal, I always think of supper at Grandpa's house. Juicy steak or chicken perfectly fried, mashed potatoes, pickles, and—my favorite—baked beans and cornbread. One of the first things I really bonded over with Grandpa was the fact that nobody else in the family really seems to be a fan of pickles, but Grandpa knew he could always pass them over to me and share his enjoyment of pickles with at least one person at the table. In terms of food, I can't talk about Grandpa without mentioning Crackerjacks, the gift he would send away with us every time we left the ranch. Grandpa even sent a regular shipment of Crackerjacks to me while I was in Italy, and I always felt closer to home when a new box would arrive in the mail.

Besides getting to explore the ranch and eat a hearty meal, the magic of going out to visit Grandpa was in the talks we had as a family sitting around the dinner table. Some days, we'd get a lesson in history on Eagle Woman or Sacagawea, other days we'd hear stories of Grandpa's time in the navy, and sometimes he'd ask us about our lives and give us advice based off of his past experiences. My favorite of his navy stories is the day that Grandpa spent with a nice little girl in Naples.

The advice that I've appreciated the most from Grandpa is to go to school to learn, not just as a stepping stone towards a future career. Even just hearing about how Grandpa lived his life inspires me. He's taught me to work hard but work for myself, to love animals and cherish the time I spend in nature, to respect those that are older than me but remain honest about who I am. During my brattier phases growing up, Grandpa could always keep me in line and remind me of the importance of manners.

Along with spending time at his ranches, I also got to travel with Grandpa and often his girlfriend on family vacations. I absolutely adored every moment spent at the Halekulani Hotel in Honolulu with them, eating fresh mango at the breakfast buffet and walking straight out of the hotel to Waikiki Beach. Staying at that hotel was when I was lucky enough to first experience luxury and also to get my first taste of fresh papaya, which is now my favorite fruit. There was also the trip to San Diego with Grandpa, watching horse races, looking at sailboats in the marina, and eating at Grandpa's favorite diner in La Jolla. Grandpa definitely knew how to travel in style!

Thinking about Grandpa, I know that having him as a grandfather was one of the biggest blessings in my life. I am proud to be a Shultz, at least by middle name, and to know that I come from a family of successful, intelligent, hard-working people. Even more than that, Grandpa gave me a head start in life through his incredible generosity and the values of success and independence that he has instilled in me. I know that Grandpa sacrificed a lot and dedicated many years of his life to work, and through that he has been able to provide for an entire family. So I want to take this as a time to thank him for that, and also just to thank him for having been such a great grandpa.

~Summer

Grandpa celebrated eighty-nine trips around the sun. During those roughly nine decades, my grandpa, Robert Shultz, was a sailor, a businessman, a rancher, a husband, a friend, a father, and a grandfather, to name a few. Among those things, though, he was life. His outgoing, sincere nature provided for some of the best of times—stories, parties, trips, holidays, and more. My grandpa epitomized energy and passion: his ambition and spirit carried him through all his endeavors. He lived a life of undeniable success. His presence alone was enough to inspire, and he has always been one of my most cherished of role models.

There are certain hallmarks about my grandpa that I will always remember. His passion for history, politics, football, geography, livestock, music, and people made up part of his unique personality. His cooking, similarly, will always stick in my memory. The beans, chicken, cornbread, and the hearty shot of tomato juice contributed to his delicious repertoire. His cuisine—the center of many of our social gatherings—was not only a pleasure, but also a source of life. Grandpa probably held that the best kinds of food are those shared amongst family and friends—preferably not of country club origin. (That's supposed to be funny.)

Our trips to his favorite Hawaiian hotel, the Halekulani, are firmly planted in my memory as some of the best of times. The beautiful ocean, sunsets, hula dancers, and the tropic serenity are gifts I never would have been granted without him. Similarly, visiting his ship, the USS Missouri, at Pearl Harbor, was always a cool experience. He never left without a couple photos capturing his signature greeting—his feet firmly planted, his hat raised high in the air, and his left hand resting confidently in his pant pocket. He took this confident disposition everywhere he went.

His light by itself was enough to spark vitality and motivation in any of us. So how do I condense such an exuberant character to a single page? Frankly, I can't. The mark he has left on my life and all those he has touched is far too expansive for even a book to begin to capture. My grandpa's name alone best represents him. He was a man who blessed our lives just by living, just by doing it his way. And for that I am forever grateful.
~Liberty

Bob on ship

My girls both had a little more than two decades of knowing and experiencing their grandpa. Since I never met my dad's father, my wish that my girls would personally know their grandfather came true. My dad set many good examples for my girls and me. The time my kids had with him will affect their choices and perhaps the lives of future generations as my daughters have the opportunity to share and teach the lessons and passions he instilled in them.

Another part of my dad's legacy is the ranchland he left for the public to enjoy. He loved the wide-open space with a view of Pike's Peak and the historical nature of the property, with a house and barn dating back to the late 1800s. He saw nearby properties being sold to housing developments due to their proximity to Denver. He could not bear the thought of this encroaching development carving up his ranch. At the age of seventy-five, after a twenty-year ranching life, he decided in 2000 to sell his ranch to Douglas County Open Space and move into true retirement. He ensured his ranch to Douglas County Open Space to preserve the land to wildlife and western history. He wanted the ranch to remain undeveloped and open to horseback rides, hikes, picnics, and historical tours.

Douglas County allowed my dad to continue to reside in the house he built on the hill overlooking the old farmhouse, outbuildings, barn, meadow, pond, and a distant Pike's Peak. He remained there until age eighty-nine when in late July 2015 an ambulance took him to a hospital in the nearby town of Parker.

Over the years of living on Prairie Canyon Ranch, he had many visitors and a few big parties that he liked to call "blasts" or "blowouts." Douglas County allowed a "Last Blast" for his celebration of life event in June 2016. I am sure Dad was pleased with the location selection. A museum was created in the old historic farmhouse. His ashes were spread at this ranch as well as in South Dakota where he grew up.

My dad set high moral standards for me to live by. He taught my daughters and me character. He wasn't a perfect man, but he had integrity. He lived hard, played hard, and the end of his life was hard. He had survived a world war but not the indignities of old age.

I see Dad in the hereafter, riding his favorite horse, Gambler, feeding his Longhorn steers, petting his dog Buddie, and doing some jitterbug. He will be missed and definitely remembered.

Bob riding his horse Gambler

Bob feeds his steer

CHAPTER THIRTY-ONE

Death is Nothing At All

In the months after his passing, I discovered a piece that moved me profoundly. It was written by Henry Scott Holland (January 27, 1847 – March 17, 1918), who was the Regius Professor of Divinity at the University of Oxford.

> *Death is nothing at all. It does not count. I have only slipped away into the next room. Nothing has happened. Everything remains exactly as it was. I am I, and you are you, and the old life that we lived so fondly together is untouched, unchanged. Whatever we were to each other, that we are still. Call me by the old familiar name. Speak of me in the easy way which you always used. Put no difference into your tone.*

Wear no forced air of solemnity or sorrow. Laugh as we always laughed at the little jokes that we enjoyed together. Play, smile, think of me, pray for me. Let my name be ever the household word that it always was. Let it be spoken without an effort, without the ghost of a shadow upon it. Life means all that it ever meant. It is the same as it ever was. There is absolute and unbroken continuity. What is this death but a negligible accident? Why should I be out of mind because I am out of sight? I am but waiting for you, for an interval, somewhere very near, just round the corner. All is well. Nothing is hurt; nothing is lost. One brief moment and all will be as it was before. How we shall laugh at the trouble of parting when we meet again!

CHAPTER THIRTY-TWO

A Few More Thoughts

"Do all the good you can, By all the means you can,
In all the ways you can, In all the places you can,
At all the times you can, To all the people you can,
As long as ever you can."
John Wesley

My divorce in 1999 and my dad's death in 2015 were troubling times for me. But those events brought me the most personal growth. After my dad's death, I pondered how I missed the chance to say goodbye when we had years of progressive decline towards the end. Even though I cannot replay those last weeks or our final day together, I can share our story and what I learned.

With the increasing lifespan of Americans due to medical advances, many people have lost touch with the dying process. Prolongation of life appears to permeate current medical training, with its focus on the latest new treatment, drug remedy, or surgery. American society seems to fear death with crazes of exercise, supplements, special diets, and all sorts of concoctions and procedures to stave it off for as long as possible. I am not knocking advances that provide a healthier life and alleviate suffering or unnecessary premature death. I am advocating inclusion of education on end-of-life matters and the promotion of understanding, conversation, and planning.

It behooves me to remember as I advance in age that death is an inevitable part of the life cycle rather than a medical failure. I will strive for communication with doctors to better understand risks and likely outcomes of possible treatments. I will keep in mind quality over quantity of time. I may think twice about life-prolonging measures if they are likely to create more physical or emotional pain and trauma to my family as well as myself. Kathy Kalina says, "Doctors have a tendency to think of death as a personal enemy, and that's usually good. If I have an illness that can be cured, I want my doctor to wage all-out war against it. But once it becomes evident that treatment is not going to be successful, I want to spend my last days in comfort and peace."

By seizing every opportunity for kindness, forgiveness, healing, and love that crosses my path each day, I hope that my death, although perhaps sad for some, will be gracefully concluded. If I know that death is approaching, I will aim for meaningful closure and final goodbyes as best I am able.

In Dr. Byock's *The Four Things That Matter Most,* he states, "When you love someone, it is never too soon to say, 'I love you,' or premature to say, 'Thank you,' 'I forgive you,' or 'Will you please forgive me?' When there is nothing of profound importance left unsaid, relationships tend to take on an aspect of celebration, as they should." When I elect to say what needs to be said with each interaction today and when

I use the four statements regularly as opportunities present themselves, I have the chance to create deeper connections now and potentially less moments of regret upon my death.

Dr. Byock punctuates his point, stating, "I think people who are dying have a responsibility to help reconcile strained relations they have with family and previously close friends. In other words, if a relative or friend is open, it seems irresponsible to ignore the chance to heal wounded relationships before one's death."

The feeling of lack of full closure with my dad is a catalyst for me to make adjustments in my life. I search for unfinished business and do my best to complete it. Examples for me are finishing photo albums, putting my financial affairs and estate plans in order, and getting rid of stuff I don't use or enjoy. I carve out time to talk about important matters with those I love. I practice taking steps to wrap up loose ends whenever I become aware of them. I shuffle my priorities with the end in mind.

Sometimes one has time to prepare for death because of a diagnosis of cancer or some other terminal disease. Perhaps this knowledge might help to get things done or say things that need to be said. I don't know if I might suddenly die today or tomorrow. By acknowledging my impermanence, I can consider if there is anything I can do now to help my loved ones who will be left behind cope with losing me and to facilitate healing.

Contemplating my inevitable death has the potential to change a conversation the next time I see someone I love. It may provoke me to make a phone call. It may behoove me to write a letter. I can also insert a message in my "Upon Death" notebook. Because my closest relationships invariably include some conflict, misunderstandings, and hurt, as well as great love, those I leave behind might need help with forgiveness. My words or letters might pave the path to living with fewer negative emotions that might weigh down my loved ones as they live beyond me.

I wish to let my family and friends know that a disagreement or sharp words last spoken do not reflect our overall relationship. An argument is tiny in comparison to the love we shared. I encourage my loved ones to reflect on the special times and the bigger picture of our time together. Remembering special moments might soothe their loss a bit and help shift their memories to better ones.

Dr. Byock eloquently captures my hopes. "I've decided that by continuing to practice the Four Things, my relationships will, hopefully, grow stronger and more loving. If I can become the change I wish to see, my friends and family may take notice and respond in kind. And maybe, by earnestly practicing forgiveness, gratitude, and love now, I'll be adept before it's time to say my last goodbye."

When I look back on the fifty-two years my dad was alive and in my life, I feel very blessed. He provided me with a solid childhood foundation, educational opportunities, financial security, a chance to travel, and a high standard of integrity by which to live my life. He was a leader—charismatic, strong, opinionated, honest, success-driven, and family-oriented. He set a high bar and modeled mostly good examples to live by. I am grateful to have had him as my dad.

What would I have wanted to say if I had had the opportunity to see him one more time? I would like to think that I would have kept it simple and said, "I love you," then just held his hand in silence, letting that thought linger in the space of the time we had left together.

Bob and his signature pose

PART THREE

Tips, Suggestions,
and Resources

"To know what we do not know is the beginning of wisdom."
Maha Sthavira Sangharakshita

Checklist of How to Prepare Well for Your Own Death

"Maturity begins to grow when you can sense your concern for others out-weighing your concern for yourself."
John MacNoughton

My dad planned for his death in terms of documentation. I am grateful for his consideration and thoughtfulness with organizing important papers and ensuring that I had access to them. I consider his foresight in this area a gift to me. I used his example to prepare documents for my own eventual death in order to assist my daughters with the same courtesy. I created a list and am sharing it here for your reference.

1. Create an "Upon Death or Estate" notebook. Leave it where others can easily find it and let a few key people know its location.
2. Write a foundational draft obituary of yourself. Indicate, if you wish, that it can be expanded or edited.

3. List all key contacts and institutions, such as accountant, financial planner, attorney, bank accounts, etc.

4. Leave passwords of accounts, such as email, social media, etc., so that someone can enter and shut down or notify others of your death.

5. Leave reminders on how to reduce the chance of identity theft upon your death, such as notifying credit agencies. Instruct your relatives to request a "deceased—do not issue credit" flag be placed on your credit file.

6. If not included in another document, state your end-of-life wishes, such as burial versus cremation, where to spread ashes, music to be played at your funeral or celebration-of-life event, and any other detail that is important to you. You can also suggest a funeral home of your preference and visit it to set up arrangements of your choosing.

7. Consider writing a letter to key loved ones telling them how much they have meant to you, what you enjoyed about them, and your wish for their future. Ideally, you have told them these things verbally, but in case you have not or want them to have a written letter to keep, this is a great place to put it and the time to do it.

8. Create or update a will or trust. You can hire an estate planner to assist you or purchase software such as *Quicken WillMaker Plus* or go online to sites such as www.nolo.com.

If the language of end-of-life documents is unclear to you, here are a few phrases you might encounter in your paperwork preparation.

Advance Directive
This document explains what type of medical care you would want in the event you are unable to speak for yourself. It also indicates who would speak for you if this happened. Advance Directives usually come in the form of a Living Will and a Health Care Proxy. These documents can be prepared at any age and can ease the minds of those who might have difficult decisions to make.

Living Will
This document explains what your wishes are for medical care. Are there procedures you would want and are there ones you wish to avoid?

Health Care Proxy or Medical Durable Power of Attorney
This form says who you want to have authority and make medical decisions for you.

CPR (Cardio-Pulmonary Resuscitation) Directive and DNR (Do Not Resuscitate)
A CPR Directive allows you, or your agent, guardian, or Proxy Decision Maker on your behalf, to refuse resuscitation. CPR is an attempt to revive someone whose heart and/or breathing has stopped by using special drugs and/or machines or by firmly and repeatedly pressing the chest.

A DNR order is an order written in your medical chart by your doctor while you are being cared for in a healthcare facility, such as a hospital or nursing home.

According to the information contained within the Colorado Hospital Association's booklet entitled "Your Right to Make Healthcare Decisions," fewer than one in ten elderly, frail, or seriously ill persons will survive a resuscitation attempt; if they do survive, they might end up with traumatic injuries or brain damage. http://www.cha.com/

Each state or province has different forms, terms, and rules, so check to make sure you have documents for your country and area. www.getpalliativecare.org

Once these forms are completed, provide them to your primary doctor and key family members. These forms might need to travel with you to the hospital or care facility and be available to family in a notebook or shared electronic file.

Tips for Dealing with Your Aging Parents

*"If you love somebody, you will be a caregiver.
If you live long enough, you'll need one."*
Peter Rosenberger

Because no two personalities or histories are identical, dealing with an aging parent is a unique experience. Nonetheless, there are some basic principles that can be helpful as you navigate a similar journey. In reading sage advice coupled with going through the process of being a shepherd through my dad's decline and ultimately his death, I decided to summarize those concepts that assisted me. Some of what is outlined below I did well and some not so well. Perhaps the list will resonate with you and you can incorporate these principles in your own situation.

Accept what is. Be less invested in the ideal way to age and how it should look and practice more acceptance of the reality. Avoid the tendency to judge and blame, because it does not change the situation. Allow the parent to be as they are now. It is their journey, not yours.

Ask about your parents' wishes early. If your parents are still independent, ask them if they foresee themselves moving into a senior community. Do they wish to stay at home with homecare or live-in help? What are their hopes and expectations? Do they want life-prolonging care, limited medical care, or comfort care? Engage in conversation to uncover their wishes and revisit the questions as their health changes.

Hear what your loved one really needs. Instead of doing what you think they need, double check the wishes of your parent if they are able to communicate. There may be a large gap in perceived needs. Moving ahead without verifying what your loved one wants can cause additional duress for everyone. By checking in with your parent, you can avoid the need to back pedal or apologize later when their desires clash with your unchecked actions.

Listen. Deep, compassionate listening can help relieve suffering. In conversation, if you don't know what to say, simply listen and be with them. If perseveration or inappropriate verbalization crops up, it may be prudent to change the subject or exit the room.

Put documents in order. Does your parent have a standard or living will, advanced directives, end-of-life medical wishes, healthcare proxies, medical power of attorney? Where are their documents located? Do you have copies? Have you created these items for yourself too?

Prepare for death. Does your parent wish to be buried or cremated? What other end-of-life decisions can be handled or discussed now? Do you have handy phone contact information to notify professionals as well as family and friends when death occurs? Do you have this matter prepared for yourself as well?

Create Lists. Compile lists of bank accounts, financial institutions and investments, advisors, doctors, medications, allergies, and other important people and issues that will come in handy when the need arises. Update these lists annually or whenever changes occur for your parent and yourself and keep them in a place where you have access and others can find them easily.

Remember that little things add up. Sometimes little things mean more to your parent than you might think. Showing your loved one a picture that might please them, massaging a sore spot, reading to them, or bringing a favorite food item can make a difference, even if it seems a small gesture to you.

Gather support. Create a network of neighbors, friends, family, and agencies that can work together for the care of a parent. Communicate within the group to keep everyone up to date and apprised of changes and current and/or anticipated needs. Reach out to agencies such as hospice when you need more help.

When reporting to relatives and friends, state what is going well first. Observing, focusing, and sharing what is working can buffer the less optimal news that comes subsequently. Look for some good news to share.

Create memory and scrap books. Compile special photographs, recipes, and stories in a book that can be shared and enjoyed now and as a keepsake for after death. Chip away at the collection to honor the life and legacy of your parent. Utilize professionals to assist you if your time is limited.

Write love letters. Encourage or assist your parent in writing love letters to those they care about in their lives. These letters might be to their kids, grandkids, or friends whom they wish to say a few kind words about, expressing what they mean to them. These letters can heal and leave a special lasting legacy to those left behind at the time of passing. Consider writing your letters now too.

Practice giving and receiving. Your parent might be painfully aware that you are giving more than they are able to reciprocate. This imbalance may be a heavy burden to them. Anything you can do that fosters more balance between giving and receiving may be helpful to you both.

Maintain boundaries. You still have your own life to live and other roles to play. At times you will have to say "no" or "not now" to keep balance and health in your life. You may have to reclaim power that might be slipping away by asserting your needs as well. Give yourself permission to say no at times and hold your ground.

Drop the guilt. Forgive yourself and forgive your parent. You are both doing the best you can under challenging circumstances. Be kind to yourself, nurture yourself, and ask for assistance to support you through this phase of life.

Remember to breathe. Deep breathing will calm you when you are feeling fearful or anxious. Place your hand on your lower belly and count to four while slowing breathing in and watching your hand rise. Then to another count of four, slowly exhale all the air completely. Repeat several times.

Find some humor. Laughter will help you lighten stress and worry. If you cannot laugh at the moment, have a funny book to read or a movie to watch later to unwind. Tune into your favorite comedian. Ellen DeGeneres often makes me chuckle. She said, "My grandmother started walking five miles a day when she was sixty. She's ninety-seven now, and we don't know where the hell she is."

Play a game or read to your parent. Play a game of cards or checkers to pass the time and stimulate the mind. Read a book you like or an old favorite of theirs to your parent. If their hearing and mind can appreciate it, invest in audiobooks that can be played when you are not there.

Remember to take it a day at a time. Worrying about tomorrow does not help you to live in peace today. Have plans in place to navigate future contingencies and then do your best to think only of what can be done today and let tomorrow come as it will.

View the situation as an opportunity for spiritual growth. Instead of focusing solely on the ordeal or only on the perspective of loss, explore the spiritual aspect of the unfolding events.

Realize that there may be frequent ups and downs by the week, day, or hour. Avoid the poles of catastrophic or hopeful thinking that may drain your energy and lead to false conclusions. Brace for the ups and downs and have patience as you swing through the stages.

Wait before responding. Often you will need to pause before responding to avoid knee-jerk reactions or regrets. Perhaps go and take a drink of water before you answer. If tension is high, consider taking a walk to blow off steam, giving yourself even more time to compose your thoughts and words.

Seek healthy stress relief. Your body may accumulate stress in muscles, creating soreness, headaches, and back pain. Consider scheduling a massage, acupuncture, or chiropractic appointment. Avoid the buildup of ailments with treatments that align, balance, and replenish your body.

Depart from visits thoughtfully. Because you never know if your loved one might die suddenly, grab chances to express love and heartfelt goodbyes at each departure.

And finally, **allow yourself and your parent to be imperfect.** Even for an organized person, decline and death rarely proceed perfectly according to plan. And there may be no plan at all if death is sudden or if there was a refusal to prepare. Unexpected things happen. So I circle back to the first tip: **accept what is.**

Questions for Personal Reflections or Group Discussions

Family History/Upbringing/Influences

1. What do you know about your family history? Is family history important to you? If your parents have already passed, what questions do you wish you had asked them?

2. In considering the times, events, heritage, culture, etc. that shaped your parents, do you better understand their personality, behavior, values, strengths, and shortcomings? What factors have most shaped you?

3. Do you have fond memories of your own childhood or is your childhood a source of pain? Good or bad, how have your childhood experiences affected

your life today? If you raised children, how did your childhood impact your parenting style?

4. What quirk, irritating or amusing, does your parent have, or did your parent have, throughout life or at the end of life? Are you able to laugh about it? What trait do you have that might be grating or funny to your kids or family when you become older?

5. What lasting memories have lingered most after the passing of a parent or loved one?

6. What did that person teach you?

The Stuff We Accumulate

1. Have you ever had to clean out a parent's house after death or after a permanent move to a nursing home? How did the experience impact you? Did it create any personal change with regard to your own home?

2. Whose responsibility do you believe it is to deal with the stuff we accumulate? Do you tidy regularly or leave it for another day or for another person to handle? Why or why not?

End of Life Preparation

1. Have you had end-of-life conversations with a parent or loved one? How did honest dialogue affect the end? What questions do you believe are most important to ask? Are you willing to have those conversations with your family?

2. If your parents grew old and had time to prepare for their deaths, did they acknowledge or deny their mortality? How did either perspective impact their final days or the rest of the family?

3. Have you ever had to choose a nursing home or rehabilitation/care facility? If so, what did you learn from the experience?

4. Does being aware of death and your mortality change the way you live today? Has there been a particular death of a friend or family member that provoked a change for you? If so, what is that change?

5. Have you written your own obituary? If so, how was the experience?

6. Have you created documents such as Advanced Directives, Living Wills, Healthcare Proxies, and Durable Powers of Attorney? Do you have an estate plan? If not, why not?

7. Do you have your financial affairs in order?

8. Does your family know your wishes on items such as burial or cremation and wishes for services or a celebration-of-life event? Have you made funeral requests or arrangements?

9. Does your family know if you prefer life-prolonging care, limited medical care, or comfort care?

10. What is important to you as you age?

Dying Process/Death

1. Do you understand or have you witnessed the dying process? Is it helpful to know more about the changes that occur during decline and approaching death?

2. Have you been present at a death that was gentle, peaceful, holy, or sacred? Have you seen a difficult, traumatic, or painful death? If so, what was it like and how did it affect you?

3. Have you ever had a near death experience? If so, how has it affected you?
4. Do you fear death? If so, what aspect scares you?
5. Where would you like to die if you had a choice and who would be present, if anyone?
6. If you were on your deathbed, what might be most important to you?
7. What would be an acceptable way for you or a loved one to die?

Loss, Grief, Forgiveness, Recovery

1. How did you navigate loss and grief of a parent/loved one? Do you have any advice for others?
2. What helps you most to unwind and revitalize under stressful situations or in recovery following a death of a loved one?
3. What has helped you achieve closure from previous losses?
4. Is forgiveness an issue for you? Do you forgive easily or hold on to resentments? How does either decision affect your life? Who in your life is the most difficult to forgive and why?
5. Are you able to forgive yourself? What is hard for you to forgive about yourself?
6. With whom might you practice the *Four Most Important Things* by Dr. Ira Byock? Please forgive me, I forgive you, thank you, and I love you.

End of Life Issues

1. Have you had experience with dementia, Alzheimer's, or mental decline with your parents? What was the hardest part of your parent's loss of mental functioning? Do you have any tips to offer to others who may have a parent in the midst of this situation or at the beginnings of decline?
2. With the financial costs of healthcare and end-of-life care, do finances affect your decisions for your own future or have finances been a factor with your parents?
3. What age is ideal to die? Do you have a number in mind? If so, what and why?
4. What does a good death or bad death mean to you? Is a good death possible and, if so, how?
5. What changes in the healthcare system would you like to see?

Spiritual Matters

1. What are your beliefs about the afterlife? Do these beliefs give you comfort?
2. Have you ever experienced symbolic dreams about a lost loved one? What did the dream reveal to you?
3. Do you believe in coincidence? If so, what is a coincidence that you have experienced and what insight did you gain from it?
4. Do you have a book, passage, poem, music, or some other item that relates to death that gives you comfort or solace?

Further Reflection and Action Steps

1. If you have already lost a parent but had known from the beginning of their decline how their story would eventually end, what would you have done differently?
2. What is your philosophy of quality vs. quantity time? Have you ever missed out on quality time by pursuing treatment?
3. Have you ever asked an ill or aged loved one what their understanding of their disease or condition is?
4. Has reading this book or others like it prompted a new direction for you?
5. Have you made any changes in focus, gratitude, health, travel, relationships, conversations, etc.?

List action items or steps this book has prompted you to make.

_____

_____

_____

_____

_____

_____

_____

_____

To receive a free, printable list of these questions, visit www.LisaJShultz.com and visit resources tab.

Postscript

*"In one sense, the real reason that thousands
upon thousands of Americans still die badly
is that we collectively allow it to happen."
Ira Byock, M.D.*

From reading Dr. Byock's book *The Best Possible Care*, I have become a fan of palliative care. His book helped me understand the palliative approach to foster quality life, comfort at the end of life, and the prospect of gentle death. Reading his accounts of patient stories showed me the power of addressing the end of life with family and a medical care team working together. In our western culture, talking about death can be taboo, avoided or postponed until later, if ever, and some people seem scared to acknowledge their mortality. It would be ideal if discussions could take place while family members are still in good health and clear mental function. Otherwise, wishes and plans will most likely not be clarified and in place for the time when change inevitably occurs.

While in the midst of crisis in an emergency room or after the onset of dementia are not the times to figure things out.

Byock advocates for transformation in the way we conclude life in America. He says, "How we die is already a public health crisis, and care of people through the end of life is poised to become a generation-long social catastrophe." He further states, "The way many Americans die remains a national disgrace."

If each individual prepares for their end of life to the best of their abilities, that preparation might promote a smoother process if or when hospitalization or illness occurs.

It might behoove all of us to take it a step further and influence social change. Dr. Byock states, "For the magnitude of change that is needed to occur, social activism is necessary." This cause may not appeal to everyone, but it is one I embrace.

It is possible to achieve greater peace, healing, and closure at the end of life. My hope is that this book has increased your awareness of the potential for a dignified and graceful conclusion of life. My final offering: grab a chance to say goodbye if you are given the opportunity!

Resources

"As long as you live, keep learning how to live."
Seneca

BOOKS

Caregiver Support

Jacobs, Barry J., PsyD. *The Emotional Survival Guide for Caregivers: Looking After Yourself and Your Family While Helping an Aging Parent.* New York: Guilford Press, 2006.

Rosenberger, Peter. *Hope for the Caregiver: Encouraging Words to Strengthen Your Spirit.* Brentwood, Tennessee: Worthy Inspired, 2014.

Grief/Grieving

Karnes, Barbara, R.N. *My Friend, I Care: The Grief Experience.* Pamphlet edition: Barbara Karnes, 1991.

Kübler-Ross, Elisabeth and David Kessler. *On Grief and Grieving: Finding the Meaning of Grief Through the Five Stages of Loss.* New York: Scribner, 2014.

Kumar, Sameet M., PH.D. *Grieving Mindfully: A Compassionate and Spiritual Guide to Coping with Loss.* Oakland, California: New Harbinger Publications, Inc., 2005.

Organizing/Dealing with Clutter

Jay, Francine. *The Joy of Less: A Minimalist Guide to Declutter, Organize, and Simplify.* San Francisco: Chronicle Books, 2016.

Kingston, Karen. *Clear your Clutter with Feng Shui.* New York: Broadway Books, 1999.

Kondo, Marie. *The Life-Changing Magic of Tidying Up: The Japanese Art of Decluttering and Organizing.* New York: Ten Speed Press, 2014.

Kondo, Marie. *Spark Joy: An Illustrated Master Class on the Art of Organizing and Tidying Up.* New York: Ten Speed Press, 2016.

St. James, Elaine. *Simplify Your Life: 100 Ways to Slow Down and Enjoy the Things That Really Matter.* New York: Hachette Books, 1994.

The Dying Process

Kalina, Kathy. *Midwife For Souls: Spiritual Care For The Dying.* Boston: Pauline Books & Media, 2006.

Karnes, Barbara, R.N. *End of Life Guideline Series: A Compilation of Barbara Karnes Booklets [Gone From My Sight: The Dying Experience, The Eleventh Hour: A Caring Guideline for the Hours to Minutes Before Death, A Time to Live: Living with a Life-Threatening Illness].* Amazon Digital Services, 2012.

End-of-Life Issues

Butler, Katy. *Knocking on Heaven's Door: The Path to a Better Way of Death.* New York: Scribner, 2014.

Byock, Ira, M.D. *Dying Well: Peace and Possibilities at the End of Life.* New York: Riverhead Books, 1998.

Byock, Ira, M.D. *The Best Care Possible: A Physician's Quest to Transform Care Through the End of Life.* New York: Avery, 2013.

Byock, Ira, M.D. *The Four Things That Matter Most: A Book About Living.* New York: Atria Books, 2014.

Feldman, David B., PH.D., S. Andrew Lasher, Jr., M.D. *The End-of-Life Handbook: A Compassionate Guide to Connecting with and Caring for a Dying Loved One.* Oakland, California: New Harbinger Publications, 2008.

Gawande, Atul, M.D. *Being Mortal: Medicine and What Matters in the End.* New York: Metropolitan Books, 2014.

Smith, Fran and Sheila Himmel. *Changing the Way We Die: Compassionate End-of-Life Care and the Hospice Movement.* Berkeley: Viva Editions, 2013.

Volandes, Angelo E., M.D. *The Conversation: A Revolutionary Plan for End-Of-Life Care.* New York: Bloomsbury USA, 2015.

Webb, Marilyn. *The Good Death: The New American Search to Reshape the End of Life.* New York: Bantam, 1999.

Williams-Murphy, Monica, M.D. and Kristian Murphy. *It's Ok to Die.* MKN, LLC, 2011.

Spiritual

Hawkins, David R. *Letting Go: The Pathway to Surrender.* Carlsbad, California: Hay House, Inc., 2012.

Newton, Michael, PH.D. *Journey of the Souls: Case Studies of Life Between Lives.* St. Paul: Llewellyn Publications, 1996.

Newton, Michael, PH.D. *Destiny of the Souls: New Case Studies of Life Between Lives.* St. Paul: Llewellyn Publications, 2000.

Rushnell, SQuire. *When GOD Winks at You: How God Speaks Directly to You Through the Power of Coincidence.* Nashville: Thomas Nelson, 2006.

Singer, Michael A. *The Untethered Soul: The Journey Beyond Yourself.* Oakland, California: New Harbinger Publications/ Noetic Books, 2007.

Wyatt, Karen, M.D. *What Really Matters: 7 Lessons for Living from the Stories of the Dying.* New York: SelectBooks, Inc., 2011.

Wyatt, Karen M.D. *The TAO of Death: The Secret of a Rich & Meaningful Life.* CreateSpace Independent Publishing Platform, 2016.

Miscellaneous

Brown, Brené. *Daring Greatly: How the Courage to Be Vulnerable Transforms the Way We Live, Love, Parent, and Lead.* New York: Avery, 2015.

Cohen, Kerry. *The Truth of Memoir: How to Write About Yourself and Others with Honesty, Emotion, and Integrity.* Blue Ash, Ohio: Writer's Digest Books, 2014.

Brokaw, Tom. *The Greatest Generation.* New York: Random House Trade Paperbacks, 2005.

WEBSITES

End-of-Life Issues

www.agingwithdignity.org

Aging with Dignity is a national nonprofit organization with a mission to affirm and safeguard the human dignity of individuals as they age and to promote better care for those near the end of life.

www.bkbooks.com/blog

Something to Think About: a blog on end of life by Barbara Karnes.

www.changingthewaywedie.com

Website about the book, *Changing the Way We Die*, with additional resources.

www.angelovolandes.com

Physician advocate for end-of-life conversations.

www.theconversationproject.org

The Conversation Project is dedicated to helping people talk about their wishes for end-of-life care.

www.theconversationbook.org
> Video link advocating conversation and the three options of life-prolonging care, limited medical care, and comfort care.

http://deathoverdinner.org/
> The creators have gathered dozens of medical and wellness leaders to cast an unflinching eye at end of life and created an uplifting interactive adventure that transforms this seemingly difficult conversation into one of deep engagement, insight, and empowerment.

www.irabyock.org
> Dr. Ira Byock is a leading palliative care physician, author, and public advocate for improving care through the end of life.

www.karenwyattmd.com
> Her book, *What Really Matters: 7 Lessons for Living from the Stories of the Dying,* details her experiences as a hospice physician. Her book, *The TAO of Death: The Secret of a Rich & Meaningful Life* provides reflective wisdom and spirituality of the dying process.

www.eoluniversity.com
> Resources and inspiration for the end of life.

www.oktodie.com
> Their mission is to create conditions in which people: plan ahead, make their peace, understand that it is *okay to die* naturally, and make educated choices, which allow them to pass away peacefully and comfortably surrounded by those who love them most.

www.prepareforyourcare.org

A website that assists with making medical decisions for yourself and others, talk with your doctors, and get the medical care that is right for you.

www.codaalliance.org

The Coda Alliance is dedicated to helping you comfortably deal with one of life's most difficult situations—starting your end-of-life conversation. Check out the "Go Wish Game."

Forms/Planning for Death

www.mydirectives.com

MyDirectives makes it easy to create a state-of-the-art emergency, critical, and advance care plan.

www.caringinfo.org

CaringInfo, a program of the National Hospice and Palliative Care Organization, provides free resources to help people make decisions about end-of-life care and services before a crisis.

Palliative Care and Hospice

www.getpalliativecare.org

Information and resources for palliative care.

www.nhpco.org

National Hospice and Palliative Care Organization
800-658-8898

www.aarp.org/families/end_life
AARP End of Life Resources
Grief and Loss Resources
888-687-2277

Funeral/Celebration of Life Information

www.funerals.org
Funeral Consumers Alliance
800-765-0107

www.nfda.org
National Funeral Directors Association
800-228-6332

www.homefuneralalliance.org
National Home Funeral Alliance
This is the place to find information about home funerals, including directories for where to find home funeral guides, home funeral education programs, home-funeral-friendly funeral directors, celebrants, clergy, and groups who will help families when needed.

www.greenburialcouncil.org
Green Burial Council believes burial is "green" only when it furthers legitimate environmental and societal aims, such as protecting worker health, reducing carbon emissions, conserving natural resources, and preserving habitat.

www.greenburialnaturally.org
Green Burial Naturally: State-By-State Where, How, and Why to Choose Green Burial.

www.celebrationsoflife.net
Their mission is to provide a meaningful Legacy Journey® experience to help individuals and families live their lives with intention and share their values, wisdom, and generosity with loved ones and future generations.

Miscellaneous

https://www.ncoa.org/healthy-aging/falls-prevention/
Information online about Falls Prevention by the National Council on Aging.

http://www.bankrate.com/finance/debt/request-credit-freeze-for-deceased.aspx#ixzz3tHcYGuCW
How to request a credit freeze for the deceased.

Perhaps a few of these resources called to you. To read a more in-depth review of each book, visit and follow Lisa on Goodreads: https://www.goodreads.com/LisaJShultz.

If you have found or read any books or articles that you believe would be good additions to this list, please contact me at www.LisaJShultz.com. An ever-expanding and updated resource list is available on my website, thanks to the suggestions of my readers and further research since the book's publication.

Acknowledgments

*"Memoir provides a connection between the writer and reader.
A sort of intimacy is forged when someone reads your book and
both you and your reader wind up less alone in the world."*
Kerry Cohen, Author of *The Truth of Memoir*

N o names have been changed and there are no fabricated
scenes in this book. However, sibling names and photos
were removed at their request and other names were omitted
for privacy. To the best of my recollection, I have accurately
recounted dates and details. I have been mindful to bring the
story alive through my eyes only, with the exception of my
daughters' thoughts on the legacy of their grandfather. They
gave me permission to print their words and names, which I
felt brought depth to the impact he had in their lives.

I did not intend to hurt anyone in the writing of this book.
During the pre-publication process, family response was wide
and varied. Some refused to read the book and others were
ambivalent. A few family members expressed harsh words

and opinions. Others loved it and were supportive. The choice to read or not read about my dad's difficult end of life may have stirred up individual issues and emotions. Some family members did not believe that the realities and details of our dad's end of life and death should be shared with others. And some expressed graceful and valuable feedback to improve the book.

I will admit that I was not prepared for the diverse extremes of reaction. However, those reactions provided me with another learning and growth opportunity. As I worked through my feelings that the range of responses stimulated in me, I initially experienced heartbreak and another wave of loss. I then dedicated myself to understanding my family's perspectives to the best of my abilities and have attempted to heal unresolved issues as they arose within me.

The fact is that all writers experience varied reviews. We are all wired differently due to our upbringing, beliefs, individual personalities, the principles we were taught, and our personal experiences. Kerry Cohen, author of *The Truth of Memoir*, describes what to expect when publishing. "You will need to prepare yourself for the attack, because it will come. Strangers will decide you are a terrible person. They will decide they hate you, never having met you, because you are showing them parts of themselves they may not want to see. However, if you tell your truth honestly and vulnerably, you will also get messages from people—complete strangers—who are moved by your story, who see themselves in your words." Ultimately, time will tell the overall impact of this book.

I have been careful to acknowledge the books, articles, and resources that provided me with valuable education, insight, and guidance. I believe I have provided proper credit and appreciation to those authors and organizations.

In the last few years of my dad's life and acutely in the last three months in the rehab facility, T and I talked together or emailed frequently. T had lost his mother several years earlier and his father was in poor health. As a result, T shared valuable insight about end-of-life struggles in which I had no prior experience. He helped with regular visits to the hospital and rehab facility, which allowed my sister and me some much-needed breaks to rest. T and I had many late night phone conversations to rehash what was going on with my dad. T—you helped my dad and me in a big way and I am grateful.

I give a big thanks to Tim, who patiently listened to my frustrations when I returned from visits to my dad and for his unwavering support and kindness.

A special thanks to many friends and acquaintances, who gave me wise counsel and encouragement for this book.

I thank my editor Donna Mazzitelli for guiding me to present my story in an honest, honoring, and empowering way.

I appreciate Andrea Costantine Ransom for her cover design, interior layout, and behind-the-scenes timeless friendship.

Cheers to Polly Letofsky for project management assistance.

I sincerely appreciate Karen Wyatt's eloquent Foreword to introduce the book.

I thank you, my reader, who chose to read this memoir.

Finally, I thank my dad for being my teacher and dad extraordinaire.

About the Author

Lisa Shultz moved from her hometown of Denver to Breckenridge, Colorado. She is the author of *Ready or Not: Tips for the New Grad*, which was winner in the Gift Books category of the 2014 The National Indie Excellence Book Awards and finalist in the category of Career Books for the 2014 Next Generation Indie Excellence Book Awards. She has also written several other books prior to *A Chance To Say Goodbye*.

When she is not writing, Lisa can be found swimming, dancing, tending her garden, tidying her home, reading, traveling, or connecting with friends and family.

To learn more about Lisa, including how to request her for book club visits, speaking engagements, or your next group event, be sure to visit her website at www.LisaJShultz.com.

Review Request

If you found reading my book of value, I would be appreciative to receive your review on your purchase site, Goodreads, or any other review platform. By sharing your thoughts and impressions, you will help other readers determine if this book might be right for them. I sincerely thank you for your time!

~Lisa

"Here is a test to find whether your
mission on earth is finished:
If you're alive, it isn't.
From *Illusions* by Richard Bach

More Praise for
A Chance to Say Goodbye...

BlueInk Review
Reviewed: March 2017

Lisa Shultz's father died at 89, having outlived his quality of life by five years. *A Chance to Say Goodbye* is the impressive result of Shultz's considerable soul-searching about the experience.

A WWII veteran who lived alone in a remote area of Colorado, Shultz's father had lost his hearing, mobility, and autonomy. Multiple heart attacks, a stroke, a fractured hip, dementia and depression forced him off his beloved ranch and into the medical system. That, in turn, forced his daughter, a former physical therapist, into the role of decision-maker, grappling with choices that left her at odds with medical professionals who dealt with death by refusing to address it.

Conversations about her father's wishes were put off until he was incapable of having them. For Shultz, prioritizing or solving his issues became "a never-ending hopeless job." Sadly, her dad's death, from pneumonia and other complications following gall bladder surgery, brought her neither peace nor closure. Instead, she ruminated about his final days, "dark with unnecessary confusion and turmoil for him and for those he left behind," and the lessons they held.

Part tribute, part memoir, part guide, *A Chance to Say Goodbye* succeeds on all counts, with lyrical writing and thorough research. The book is divided into sections devoted to her father's life, reflections following his death, and resources for dealing with aging parents or preparing for one's own death– resources she desperately needed but didn't compile until after the fact.

In recounting her father's story, Shultz enables readers to share in her loss. And she offers a wealth of practical advice on everything from writing an obituary to clearing out a house. Shultz also writes passionately about the high cost—human and financial—of what nurses call "the million-dollar sendoff," the aggressive, hyper-medicalized care at life's end that adds neither quality nor time.

Thought provoking and absorbing, *A Chance to Say Goodbye* has much to offer readers willing to confront the challenging subject of end-of-life.

—BlueInk Review
Starred Review

Clarion Rating: ★ ★ ★ ★
Reviewed by Michelle Anne Schingler
April 6, 2017

A Chance to Say Goodbye is a heartfelt, moving reminder that loving words are never wasted.

Half a memoir, half an exploration of grief, Lisa Shultz's *A Chance to Say Goodbye* is a moving exploration of how one can best prepare to lose a loved one.

The book starts off with a family history—an exercise that may be of limited interest to those outside of the Shultz clan, but highlights the author's deep affection for her father and her sense of connection to her family's roots. Historical facts are preserved alongside family details, including information about what was going on in the years that family members were born, what was on the radio, and even who family members share their birth years with. Such qualities give the text a homey charm, and nostalgia for years gone by adds to this sweetness.

The life and death of Shultz's father, Robert, provides the impetus for this exploration of grief. The author recalls how he left rural life and fought in World War II aboard the U.S.S. Missouri. Notes from the period are preserved alongside Robert's words regarding the on-board surrender of Japan, and the retrospective warrants admiration. Shultz's pride for her father's historic achievements shines through, and her reflectiveness when it comes to old family wounds, particularly around her parents' relationship, is sobering.

"He seemed to grow kinder and gentler with age," Shultz says, and as her relationship with her father improves in her adulthood, so too does her awareness of his mortality. Family stories move forward briskly to the most challenging part of their father-daughter relationship so far: preparations for final goodbyes. Ultimately, Shultz found that avoidance came more easily than acceptance, and her chapters are a reminder that a more open kind of departure might be desirable. Blunt details about the daily implications of Robert's declining mobility are graphic but honest.

The book's pace changes when it switches to discussions of grief, affording Shultz the space to gather key moments in her mourning: the absorption of lovely scenery; the wish to reverse key moments of last exchanges. Such meditations are sympathetic, as are declarations like "deep grief is not a weakness; rather it shows that I chose to love deeply." Accounts of handling the minutia in the aftermath of loss, including cleaning out cluttered homes, are honestly rendered and easy to identify with.

The last portion of Shultz's book will prove the most relevant for those making, or helping to make, final preparations. It draws from doctors, scholars, and fellow writers to contextualize death and grief, resulting in thoughtful, helpful recommendations, with the author's own experiences drawn in as examples.

Shultz is a self-critical guide through the process of loss, but she also seems to find some peace in the idea that her insights might help others to make healthier choices. Communication stands out as an essential tool, and Shultz's preparatory notes are full of sage advice. Prose is clear and direct, and the end result is both reflective and encouraging.

A Chance to Say Goodbye is a heartfelt, moving reminder that loving words are never wasted. In its personal nature, it makes convincing arguments against risking regret.

— *Foreword* Clarion Reviews

Made in the USA
San Bernardino, CA
12 September 2017